The Twelve Testaments of Jacob's Twelve Sons

LARGE PRINT

Edited into 21st Century American English by

Pamela Ayn Austen

From the 1926 Rutherford H. Platt Jr. Translation

entirely JESUS

Published by Entirely Jesus
www.EntirelyJesus.com

© 2018 Austen
Cover Design by P.A. Austen
Cover Painting: Released by an Unknown Artist to Creative Commons CCO.

These twelve books of the Apocrypha were never in canonized Scripture, but were called pseudepigrapha, which means spurious writings that are falsely attributed to Biblical persons or times, believed to have been written around 200 BC and 200 AD. *The Forgotten Books of Eden*, by Rutherford H. Platt, Jr., (1926), which translated these ancient Jewish writings into old English is now in the public domain.

ISBN 10: 1-948229-18-8
ISBN 13: 978-1-948229-18-0

First Edition, Soft Cover, Large Print
Printed in the United States of America

Table of Contents

TESTAMENT OF REUBEN

The First-Born Son of Jacob and Leah

Chapter 1

1. THE copy of the Testament of Reuben, even the commands which he gave his sons before he died in the hundred and twenty-fifth year of his life.

2. Two years after the death of Joseph his brother, when Reuben fell ill, his sons and his sons' sons were gathered together to visit him.

3. He said to them: "My children, I am dying, and I am going the way of my fathers."

4. Seeing there Judah and Gad and Asher, his brethren, he said to them: "Raise me up that I may tell to my brethren and to my children what things I have hidden in my heart, for now, at length, I am passing away."

5. He arose and kissed them and said to them: "Hear, my brethren and my children, give ear to Reuben your father, in the commands which I give to you.

6. I call to witness against you this day the God of heaven, that you walk not in the sins of youth and fornication, wherein I was poured out and defiled the bed of my father Jacob.

7. I tell you that he smote me with a sore plague in my loins for seven months; and had not my father Jamb prayed for me to the Lord, the Lord would have destroyed me.

8. For I was thirty years old when I wrought the evil thing before the Lord, and for seven months I was sick unto death.

9. After this, I repented with set purpose of my soul for seven years before the Lord.

10. Wine and strong drink I drank not, and flesh entered not into my mouth, and I ate no pleasant food; but I mourned over my sin, for it was great, such as had not been in Israel.

11. Now hear me, my children, what things I saw concerning the seven spirits of deceit, when I repented.

12. Seven spirits therefore are appointed against man, and they are the leaders in the works of youth.

13. Seven other spirits are given to him at his creation, that through them should be done every work of man.

14. The first is the spirit of life, with which the constitution of man is created.

15. The second is the sense of sight, with which arises desire.

16. The third is the sense of hearing, with which comes teaching.

17. The fourth is the sense of smell, with which tastes are given to draw air and breath.

18 The fifth is the power of speech, with which comes knowledge.

19. The sixth is the sense of taste, with which comes the eating of meats and drinks; and by it strength is produced, for in food is the foundation of strength.

20. The seventh is the power of procreation and sexual intercourse, with which through love of pleasure, sins enter.

21. Wherefore it is the last in order of creation, and the first in that of youth, because it is filled with ignorance, and leads the youth as a blind man to a pit, and as a beast to a precipice.

22. Besides all these, there is an eighth spirit of sleep, with which is brought about the trance of nature and that of death.

23. With these spirits are mingled the spirits of error.

24. First, the spirit of fornication is seated in the nature and in the senses.

25. The second, the spirit of insatiableness in the belly.

26. The third, the spirit of fighting, in the liver and gall.

27. The fourth is the spirit of fawning flatteries and deception, that through invasive attention, one may feel they are fair and lovely.

28. The fifth is the spirit of pride, that one may be boastful and arrogant.

29. The sixth is the spirit of lying, in perdition and jealousy, to practice deceits and concealments from kindred and friends.

30. The seventh is the spirit of injustice, with which are thefts and acts of greed, that a man may fulfill the desire of his heart; for injustice works together with the other spirits by the taking of gifts.

31. With all of these, the spirit of sleep is joined, which is that of error and fantasy.

32. So perishes every young man, darkening his mind from the truth, and not understanding the law of God, nor obeying the admonitions of his fathers, as befell me also in my youth.

33. And now, my children, love the truth, and it will preserve you; hear the words of Reuben your father.

34. Pay no heed to the face of a woman,

35. Nor associate with another man's wife,

36. Nor meddle with affairs of womankind.

37. For had I not seen Bilhah bathing in a covered place, I would not have fallen into this great iniquity.

38. For my mind taking in the thought of the woman's nakedness, suffered me not to sleep until I had wrought the abominable thing.

39. For while Jacob our father had gone to Isaac his father, when we were in Eder, near to Ephrath in Bethlehem, Bilhah became drunk and was asleep uncovered in her chamber.

40. Having therefore gone in and beheld her nakedness, I wrought the impiety without her perceiving it, and leaving her sleeping departed.

41. Immediately, an angel of God revealed to my father concerning my impiety, and he came and mourned over me, and he touched her no more.

Chapter 2

1. PAY no heed, therefore, my children, to the beauty of women, nor set your mind on their affairs; but walk in singleness of heart in the fear of the Lord, and expend labor on good works and on study and on your flocks, until the Lord gives you a wife, whom He will, that you suffer not as I did.

2. For until my father's death, I had not boldness to look in his face or to speak to any of my brethren because of the reproach.

3. Even until now, my conscience causes me anguish on account of my impiety.

4. Yet my father comforted me much, and prayed for me to the Lord, that the anger of the Lord might pass from me, even as the Lord showed.

5. From then until now, I have been on my guard and have sinned not.

6. Therefore, my children, I say to you, observe all things whatsoever I command you, and you shall not sin.

7. For a pit to the soul is the sin of fornication, separating it from God, and bringing it near to idols, because it deceives the mind and understanding, and leads down young men into Hades before their time.

8. For many has fornication destroyed; because, though a man be old or noble, or rich or poor, he brings reproach upon himself with the sons of men, and derision with Satan.

9. For you heard regarding Joseph how he guarded himself from a woman, and purged his thoughts from all fornication, and found favor in the sight of God and men.

10. For the Egyptian woman did many things to him, and summoned magicians, and offered him

love potions, but the purpose of his soul admitted no evil desire.

11. Therefore, the God of your fathers delivered him from every evil and hidden death.

12. For if fornication does not overcome your mind, neither can Satan overcome you.

13. For evil are women, my children; and since they have no power or strength over man, they use wiles by outward attractions, that they may draw him to themselves.

14. Whom they cannot bewitch by outward attractions, him they overcome by craft.

15. For moreover, concerning them, the angel of the Lord told me, and taught me, that women are overcome by the spirit of fornication more than men, and in their heart, they plot against men; and by means of their adornment they deceive first their minds, and by the glance of the eye instill the poison, and then through the accomplished act, they take them captive.

16. For a woman cannot force a man openly, but by a harlot's bearing, she beguiles him.

17. Flee, therefore, fornication, my children, and command your wives and your daughters, that they adorn not their heads and faces to deceive the mind, because every woman who uses these wiles has been reserved for eternal punishment.

18. For in this way they allured the Watchers who were before the flood; for as these continually beheld them, they lusted after them, and they conceived the act in their mind; for they changed themselves into the shape of men and appeared to them when they were with their husbands.

19. The women, lusting in their minds after their forms, gave birth to giants, for the Watchers appeared to them, as reaching even unto heaven.

20. Beware, therefore, of fornication; and if you wish to be pure in mind, guard your senses from every woman.

21. Command the women likewise not to associate with men, that they also may be pure in mind.

22. For constant meetings, even though the ungodly deed is not performed, are to them an irremediable disease, and to us a destruction of Satan and an eternal reproach.

23. For in fornication, there is neither understanding or godliness, and all jealousy dwells in the lust of it.

24 Therefore, then I say to you, you will be jealous against the sons of Levi, and will seek to be exalted over them; but you shall not be able.

25. For God will avenge them, and you shall die by an evil death. For to Levi God gave the sovereignty and to Judah with him and to me also, and to Dan and Joseph, that we should be for rulers.

26. Therefore, I command you to hearken to Levi, because he shall know the law of the Lord, and shall give ordinances for judgement and

shall sacrifice for all Israel until the consummation of the times, as the anointed High Priest, of whom the Lord spoke.

27. I adjure you by the God of heaven to do truth each one unto his neighbor, and to entertain love each one for his brother.

28. Draw near to Levi in humbleness of heart, that you may receive a blessing from his mouth.

29. For he shall bless Israel and Judah, because to him has the Lord chosen to be king over all the nation.

30. Bow down before his seed, for on our behalf, it will die in wars, visible and invisible, and will be among you an eternal king."

31. Reuben died, having given these commands to his sons. They placed him in a coffin until they carried him up from Egypt and buried him in Hebron in the cave where his father was.

TESTAMENT OF SIMEON

The Second Son of Jacob and Leah

Chapter 1

1. THE copy of the words of Simeon, the things which he spoke to his sons before he died, in the hundred and twentieth year of his life, at which time Joseph, his brother, died.

2. For when Simeon was sick, his sons came to visit him, and he strengthened himself and sat up and kissed them, and said:

3. "Hearken, my children, to Simeon your father, and I will declare to you what things I have in my heart.

4. I was born of Jacob, as my father's second son, and my mother Leah called me Simeon, because the Lord had heard her prayer.

5. Moreover, I became strong exceedingly; I shrank from no achievement, nor was I afraid of

anything. For my heart was hard, and my liver was immovable, and my bowels without compassion,

6. Because valor also has been given from the Most High to men in soul and body.

7. For in the time of my youth, I was jealous in many things of Joseph, because my father loved him beyond all.

8. I set my mind against him to destroy him because the prince of deceit sent forth the spirit of jealousy and blinded my mind, so that I regarded him not as a brother, nor did I spare even Jacob my father.

9. But his God and the God of his fathers sent forth His angel, and delivered him out of my hands.

10. For when I went to Shechem to bring ointment for the flocks, and Reuben to Dothan, where were our necessaries and all our stores, Judah my brother sold him to the Ishmaelites.

11. When Reuben heard these things, he was grieved, for he wished to restore him to his father.

12. But on hearing this, I was exceedingly wroth against Judah in that he let him go away alive, and for five months, I continued wrathful against him.

13. But the Lord restrained me, and withheld from me the power of my hands; for my right hand was half withered for seven days.

14. I knew, my children, that because of Joseph, this had befallen me, and I repented and wept; and I besought the Lord God that my hand might be restored and that I might hold myself aloof from all pollution and envy and from all folly.

15. For I knew that I had devised an evil thing before the Lord and Jacob my father, on account of Joseph my brother, in that I envied him.

16. Now, my children, hearken to me and beware of the spirit of deceit and envy.

17. For envy rules over the whole mind of a man, and suffers him neither to eat or to drink, nor to do any good thing. But it ever suggests to him to destroy him that he envies; and so long as he that is envied flourishes, he that envies fades away.

18. Two years therefore I afflicted my soul with fasting in the fear of the Lord, and I learned that deliverance from envy comes by the fear of God.

19. For if a man flees to the Lord, the evil spirit runs away from him and his mind is lightened.

20. Moving forward, he sympathizes with him whom he envied and forgives those who are hostile to him, and so he ceases from his envy.

Chapter 2

1. AND my father asked concerning me, because he saw that I was sad; and I said to him, "I am pained in my liver.

2. For I mourned more than they all, because I was guilty of the selling of Joseph.

3. When we went down into Egypt, and he bound me as a spy, I knew that I was suffering justly, and I did not grieve.

4. Now Joseph was a good man, and he had the Spirit of God within him, being compassionate and pitiful, he bore no malice against me, but he loved me even as the rest of his brethren.

5. Beware, therefore, my children, of all jealousy and envy, and walk in singleness of heart, that God may give you also grace and glory and blessing upon your heads, even as you saw in Joseph's case.

6. All his days he reproached us not concerning this thing, but he loved us as his own soul, and beyond, his own sons glorified us and gave us riches and cattle and fruits.

7. Do also, my children, love each one his brother with a good heart, and the spirit of envy will withdraw from you.

8. For envy makes savage the soul and destroys the body; it causes anger and war in the mind, and stirs one up to deeds of blood, and leads the mind into frenzy, and causes tumult to the soul and trembling to the body.

9. For even in sleep, malicious jealousy gnaws, and with wicked spirits disturbs the soul, and causes the body to be troubled, and wakes the mind from sleep in confusion; and as a wicked and poisonous spirit, so appears it to men.

10. Therefore was Joseph comely in appearance and goodly to look upon, because no wickedness dwelt in him; for some of the trouble of the spirit, manifests within the face.

11. Now, my children, make your hearts good before the Lord, and your ways straight before men, and you shall find grace before the Lord and men.

12. Beware, therefore, of fornication, for fornication is mother of all evils, separating from God, and bringing near to Satan.

13. For I have seen it inscribed in the writing of Enoch that your sons shall be corrupted in fornication, and shall do harm to the sons of Levi with the sword.

14. But they shall not be able to withstand Levi; for he shall wage the war of the Lord and shall conquer all of your hosts.

15. They shall be few in number, divided in Levi and Judah, and there shall be none of you for sovereignty, even as also our father prophesied in his blessings.

Chapter 3

1. I have told you all things, that I may be acquitted of your sin.

2. Now, if you remove your envy and all unrepentance, as a rose shall my bones flourish in Israel, and as a lily my flesh in Jacob, and my odor shall be as the odor of Libanus, and as cedars shall holy ones be multiplied from me forever, and their branches shall stretch afar off.

3. Then shall perish the seed of Canaan, and a remnant shall not be unto Amalek, and all the Cappadocians shall perish, and all Hittites shall be utterly destroyed.

4. Then shall fail the land of Ham, and all the people shall perish.

5. Then shall all the earth rest from trouble, and all the world under heaven from war.

6. Then the Mighty One of Israel shall glorify Shem.

7. For the Lord God shall appear on earth, and Himself save men.

8. Then shall all the spirits of deceit be given to be trodden under foot, and men shall rule over wicked spirits.

9. Then shall I arise in Joy and will bless the Most High because of his marvelous works, because God has taken a body and eaten with men and saved men.

10. Now, my children, obey Judah, and obey Levi, and don't be lifted up against these two tribes, for from them shall arise to you the salvation of God.

11. For the Lord shall raise up from Levi, as it were, a High Priest, and from Judah as it were a King, God and man; He shall save all the Gentiles and the race of Israel.

12. Therefore, I give you these commands that you also may command your children that they may observe them throughout their generations."

13. When Simeon had made an end of commanding his sons, he slept with fathers, an hundred and twenty years old.

14. They laid him in a wooden coffin to be taken up to Hebron. They took them up secretly during a war of the Egyptians, for the bones of Joseph, the Egyptians guarded in the tombs of the kings.

15. For the sorcerers told them that on the departure of the bones of Joseph, there should be throughout all the land darkness and gloom, and an exceeding great plague to the Egyptians, so that even with a lamp, a man should not recognize his brother.

16. The sons of Simeon bewailed their father.

17. They were in Egypt until the day of their departure by the hand of Moses.

TESTAMENT OF LEVI

The Third Son of Jacob and Leah

Chapter 1

1. THE copy of the words of Levi, the things which he ordained to his sons, according to all that they should do, and what things should befall them until the day of judgement.

2. He was sound in health when he called them to him; for it had been revealed to him that he should die.

3. When they were gathered together, he said to them:

4. "I, Levi, was born in Haran, and I came with my father to Shechem.

5. I was young, about twenty years of age, when, with Simeon, I took vengeance on Hamor for our sister Dinah.

6. When I was feeding the flocks in Abel-Maul, the spirit of understand of the Lord came upon me, and I saw all men corrupting their way, and that unrighteousness had built for itself walls, and lawlessness sat upon towers.

7. I was grieving for the race of the sons of men, and I prayed to the Lord that I might be saved.

8. Then there fell upon me a sleep, and I beheld a high mountain, and I was upon it.

9. The heavens were opened, and an angel of God said to me, 'Levi, enter.'

10. I entered from the first heaven, and I saw there a great sea hanging.

11. Further I saw a second heaven far brighter and more brilliant, for there was a boundless light also therein,

12. And I said to the angel, 'Why is this so?' and the angel said to me, 'Marvel not at this, for you shall see another heaven more brilliant and incomparable.

13. When you have ascended there, you shall stand near the Lord, and you shall be His minister, and you shall declare His mysteries to men, and you shall proclaim concerning Him that shall redeem Israel.

14. And by you and Judah shall the Lord appear among men, saving every race of men.

15. From the Lord's portion shall be your life, and He shall be your field and vineyard, and fruits, gold, and silver.

16. Hear, therefore, regarding the heavens which have been shown to you.

17. The lowest is for this cause gloomy to you, in that it beholds all the unrighteous deeds of men.

18. It has fire, snow, and ice made ready for the day of judgement, in the righteous judgement of God; for in it are all the spirits of the retributions for vengeance on men.

19. In the second are the hosts of the armies which are ordained for the day of judgement, to

work vengeance on the spirits of deceit and of Satan.

20. Above them are the holy ones.

21. In the highest of all dwells the Great Glory, far above all holiness.

22. In the heaven next to it are the archangels, who minister and make propitiation to the Lord for all the sins of ignorance of the righteous;

23. Offering to the Lord a sweet smelling savor, a reasonable and a bloodless offering.

24. In the heaven below this are the angels who bear answers to the angels of the presence of the Lord.

25. In the heaven next to this are thrones and dominions, in which always they offer praise to God.

26. When, therefore, the Lord looks upon us, all of us are shaken; yes, the heavens and the earth, and the abysses are shaken at the presence of His majesty.

27. But the sons of men, having no perception of these things, sin and provoke the Most High.

Chapter 2

1. NOW, therefore, know that the Lord shall execute judgement upon the sons of men.

2. Because when the rocks are being rent, and the sun quenched, and the waters dried up, and the fire cowering, and all creation troubled, and the invisible spirits melting away, and Hades takes spoils through the visitations of the Most High, men will be unbelieving and persist in their iniquity.

3. On this account, with punishment shall they be judged.

4. Therefore the Most High has heard your prayer, to separate you from iniquity, and that you should become to Him a son and a servant and a minister of His presence.

5. The light of knowledge shall you light up in Jacob, and as the sun shall you be to all the seed of Israel.

6. There shall be given to you a blessing, and to all of your seed until the Lord shall visit all the Gentiles in His tender mercies forever.

7. Therefore, there have been given to you counsel and understanding, that you might instruct your sons concerning this;

8. Because they that bless Him shall be blessed, and they that curse Him shall perish.'

9. Thereupon the angel opened to me the gates of heaven, and I saw the holy temple, and upon a throne of glory, the Most High.

10. He said to me: 'Levi, I have given you the blessing of the priesthood until I come and sojourn in the midst of Israel.'

11. Then the angel brought me down to the earth, and gave me a shield and a sword, and said to me: 'Execute vengeance on Shechem

because of Dinah, your sister, and I will be with you because the Lord has sent me.'

12. So I destroyed at that time the sons of Hamor, as it is written in the heavenly tables.

13. I said to him: 'I pray, O Lord, tell me your name that I may call upon you in a day of tribulation.'

14. He said: 'I am the angel who intercedes for the nation of Israel that they may not be smitten utterly, for every evil spirit attacks it.'

15. After these things, I awaken and blessed the Most High, and the angel who intercedes for the nation of Israel and for all the righteous.

Chapter 3

1. WHEN I was going to my father, I found a brazen shield; and also, the name of the mountain is Aspis, which is near Gebal, to the south of Abila.

2.   I kept these words in my heart, and after this, I counselled my father and Reuben my brother, to bid the sons of Hamor not to be circumcised; for I was zealous because of the abomination which they had wrought on my sister.

3. And I slew Shechem first, and Simeon slew Hamor. After this, my brothers came and smote that city with the edge of the sword.

4. My father heard these things and was angry, and he was grieved in that they had received the circumcision, and after that had been put to death, and in his blessings, he looked amiss upon us.

5. For we sinned because we had done this thing against his will, and he was sick on that day.

6. But I saw that the sentence of God was for evil upon Shechem; for they sought to do to Sarah and Rebecca as they had done to Dinah our sister, but the Lord prevented them.

7. They persecuted Abraham our father when he was a stranger, and they vexed his flocks when

they were big with young; and Eblaen, who was born in his house, they most shamefully handled.

8. Such they did to all strangers, taking away their wives by force, and they banished them.

9. But the wrath of the Lord came upon them to the uttermost.

10. I said to my father Jacob: 'By you will the Lord despoil the Canaanites and will give their land to you and to your seed after you.'

11. For from this day forward shall Shechem be called a city of imbeciles; for as a man mocks a fool, so did we mock them.

12. Because also they had wrought folly in Israel by defiling my sister, and we departed and came to Bethel.

13. There again I saw a vision as the former, after we had spent there seventy days.

14. I saw seven men in white raiment saying to me: 'Arise, put on the robe of the priesthood,

and the crown of righteousness, and the breastplate of understanding, and the garment of truth, and the late of faith, and the turban of the head, and the ephod of prophecy.'

15. They severally carried these things and put them on me, and said to me: 'From now on, become a priest of the Lord, you and your seed forever.'

16. The first anointed me with holy oil, and gave to me the staff of judgement.

17. The second washed me with pure water, and fed me with bread and wine, even the most holy things, and clad me with a holy and glorious robe.

18. The third clothed me with a linen vestment like an ephod.

19. The fourth put around me a girdle like purple.

20. The fifth gave me a branch of rich olive.

21. The sixth placed a crown on my head.

22. The seventh placed on my head a diadem of priesthood, and he filled my hands with incense that I might serve as priest to the Lord God.

23. They said to me: 'Levi, your seed shall be divided into three offices, for a sign of the glory of the Lord who is to come.

24. And the first portion shall be great; yes, none shall be greater.

25. The second shall be in the priesthood.

26. The third shall be called by a new name, because a king shall arise in Judah and shall establish a new priesthood, after the fashion of the Gentiles.

27. His presence is beloved, as a prophet of the Most High, of the seed of Abraham our father.

28. Therefore, every desirable thing in Israel shall be for you and for your seed, and you shall eat everything fair to look upon, and the table of the Lord shall your seed apportion.

29. Some of them shall be high priests, and judges, and scribes; for by their mouth shall the holy place be guarded.'

30. When I awoke, I understood that this dream was like the first dream. I hid this also in my heart, and told it not to any man upon the earth.

31. After two days, I and Judah went up with our father Jacob to Isaac our father's father.

32. My father's father blessed me according to all the words of the visions which I had seen, and he would not come with us to Bethel.

33. When we came to Bethel, my father saw a vision concerning me, that I should be their priest to God.

34. He rose up early in the morning and paid tithes of all to the Lord through me, and so we came to Hebron to dwell there.

35. Isaac called me continually to put me in remembrance of the law of the Lord, even as the angel of the Lord showed to me.

36. He taught me the law of the priesthood of sacrifices: whole burnt-offerings, first-fruits, freewill-offerings, peace-offerings.

37. Each day he was instructing me and was busied on my behalf before the Lord, and he said to me: 'Beware of the spirit of fornication; for this shall continue and shall by your seed pollute the holy place.

38. Take, therefore, to yourself a wife without blemish or pollution, while yet you are young, and not of the race of strange nations.

39. Before entering into the holy place, bathe; and when you offer the sacrifice, wash; and again, when you finish the sacrifice, wash.

40. Of twelve trees having leaves, offer to the Lord, as Abraham taught me also.

41. Of every clean beast and bird, offer a sacrifice to the Lord.

42. Of all your first-fruits and of wine, offer the first, as a sacrifice to the Lord God, and every sacrifice, you shall salt with salt.

43. Now, therefore, observe whatsoever I command you, children; for whatsoever things I have heard from my fathers, I have declared to you.

44. And behold, I am clear from your ungodliness and transgression, which you shall commit in the end of the ages against the Savior of the world, Christ, acting godlessly, deceiving Israel, and stirring up against it great evils from the Lord.

45. You shall deal lawlessly, together with Israel, so He shall not bear with Jerusalem because of your wickedness; but the veil of the temple shall be rent, so as not to cover your shame.

46. You shall be scattered as captives among the Gentiles, and shall be for a reproach and for a curse there.

47. For the house which the Lord shall choose shall be called Jerusalem, as is contained in the book of Enoch the righteous.

48. Therefore, when I took a wife, I was twenty-eight years old, and her name was Melcha.

49. She conceived and bare a son, and I called his name Gersam, for we were sojourners in our land.

50. I saw concerning him that he would not be in the first rank.

51. Kohath was born in the thirty-fifth year of my life, towards sunrise.

52. I saw in a vision that he was standing on high in the midst of all the congregation.

53. Therefore, I called his name Kohath, which is, beginning of majesty and instruction.

54. She bare me a third son, in the fortieth year of my life; and since his mother bare him with difficulty, I called him Merari, that is, 'my bitterness,' because he also was like to die.

55. Jochebed was born in Egypt, in my sixty-fourth year, for I was renowned then in the midst of my brethren.

56. Gersam took a wife, and she bare to him Lomni and Semei. The sons of Kohath: Ambram, Issachar, Hebron, and Ozeel. The sons of Merari: Mooli, and Mouses.

57. In the ninety-fourth year, Ambram took Jochebed my daughter to him for a wife, for they were born in one day, he and my daughter.

58. Eight years old was I when I went into the land of Canaan, and eighteen years when I slew Shechem, and at nineteen years I became priest, and at twenty-eight years I took a wife, and at forty-eight I went into Egypt.

59. My children, you are a third generation. In my hundred and eighteenth year Joseph died.

Chapter 4

1. NOW, my children, I command you: Fear the Lord your God with your whole heart, and walk in simplicity according to all of His law.

2. Also teach your children letters, that they may have understanding all their life, reading unceasingly the law of God.

3. For everyone that knows the law of the Lord shall be honored, and shall not be a stranger wheresoever he goes.

4. Yes, many friends shall he gain more than his parents, and many men shall desire to serve him, and to hear the law from his mouth.

5. Work righteousness, therefore, my children, upon the earth, that you may have it as a treasure in heaven.

6. Sow good things in your souls, that you may find them in your life.

7. But if you sow evil things, you shall reap every trouble and affliction.

8. Get wisdom in the fear of God with diligence; for though there will be a leading into captivity, and cities and lands be destroyed, and gold and silver and every possession perish, the wisdom of the wise no one can take away, save the

blindness of ungodliness, and the callousness that comes of sin.

9. For if one keeps himself from these evil things, then even among his enemies shall wisdom be a glory to him, and in a strange country a fatherland, and in the midst of foes shall prove a friend.

10. Whosoever teaches noble things and does them, shall be enthroned with kings, as was also Joseph my brother.

11. Therefore, my children, I have learned that at the end of the ages, you will transgress against the Lord, stretching out hands to wickedness against Him; and to all the Gentiles shall you become a scorn.

12. For our father Israel is pure from the transgressions of the chief priests, [who shall lay their hands upon the Savior of the world].

13. For as the heaven is purer in the Lord's sight than the earth, so also be you, the lights of Israel, are purer than all the Gentiles.

14. But if you are darkened through transgressions, what, therefore, will all the Gentiles do, living in blindness?

15. Yes, you shall bring a curse upon our race, because the light of the law which was given to lighten every man, this you desire to destroy by teaching commandments contrary to the ordinances of God.

16. The offerings of the Lord you shall rob, and from His portion shall you steal choice portions, eating them contemptuously with harlots.

17. Out of covetousness, you shall teach the commandments of the Lord, wedded women shall you pollute, and the virgins of Jerusalem shall you defile; and with harlots and adulteresses shall you be joined, and the daughters of the Gentiles shall you take to wife, purifying them with an unlawful purification; and your union shall be like Sodom and Gomorrah,

18. You shall be puffed up because of your priesthood, lifting yourselves up against men,

and not only so, but also against the commands of God.

19. For you shall hold in contempt the holy things with jests and laughter.

20. Therefore, the temple, which the Lord shall choose, shall be laid waste through your uncleanness, and you shall be captives throughout all nations.

21. You shall be an abomination to them, and you shall receive reproach and everlasting shame from the righteous judgement of God.

22. All who hate you shall rejoice at your destruction.

23. If you were not to receive mercy through Abraham, Isaac, and Jacob, our fathers, not one of our seed should be left upon the earth.

24. Now I have learned that for seventy weeks you shall go astray, and profane the priesthood, and pollute the sacrifices.

25. You shall make void the law, and set as nothing the words of the prophets by evil perverseness.

26. You shall persecute righteous men, and hate the godly; the words of the faithful shall you abhor.

27. A man who renews the law in the power of the Most High, you shall call a deceiver; and at last, you shall rush upon him to slay him, not knowing his dignity, taking innocent blood through wickedness upon your heads.

28. Your holy places shall be laid waste even to the ground because of him.

29. You shall have no place that is clean; but you shall be among the Gentiles a curse and a dispersion until He shall again visit you, and in pity shall receive you through faith and water.

Chapter 5

1. WHEREAS you have heard concerning the seventy weeks, hear also concerning the priesthood. For in each jubilee, there shall be a priesthood.

2. In the first jubilee, the first who is anointed to the priesthood shall be great, and shall speak to God as to a father.

3. His priesthood shall be perfect with the Lord, and in the day of his gladness, shall he arise for the salvation of the world.

4. In the second jubilee, he that is anointed shall be conceived in the sorrow of beloved ones; and his priesthood shall be honored and shall be glorified by all.

5. The third priest shall he taken hold of by sorrow.

6. The fourth shall be in pain, because unrighteousness shall gather itself against him exceedingly, and all Israel shall hate each one his neighbor.

7. The fifth shall be taken hold of by darkness. Likewise also the sixth and the seventh.

8. In the seventh shall be such pollution as I cannot express before men, for they shall know it who do these things.

9. Therefore, shall they be taken captive and become a prey, and their land and their substance shall be destroyed.

10. In the fifth week, they shall return to their desolate country, and shall renew the house of the Lord.

11. In the seventh week, they shall become priests who are idolaters, adulterers, lovers of money, proud, lawless, lascivious, abusers of children and beasts.

12. After their punishment shall have come from the Lord, the priesthood shall fail.

13. Then shall the Lord raise up a new priest.

14. To him all the words of the Lord shall be revealed; and he shall execute a righteous

judgement upon the earth for a multitude of days.

15. His star shall arise in heaven as of a king,

16. Lighting up the light of knowledge as the sun the day, and he shall be magnified in the world.

17. He shall shine forth as the sun on the earth, and shall remove all darkness from under heaven, and there shall be peace in all the earth.

18. The heavens shall exult in his days, and the earth shall be glad, and the clouds shall rejoice;

19. And the knowledge of the Lord shall be poured forth upon the earth, as the water of the seas;

20. And the angels of the glory of the presence of the Lord shall be glad in him.

21. The heavens shall be opened, and from the temple of glory shall come upon him sanctification, with the Father's voice as from Abraham to Isaac.

22. The glory of the Most High shall be uttered over him, and the spirit of understanding and sanctification shall rest upon him in the water.

23. For he shall give the majesty of the Lord to His sons in truth forevermore;

24. And there shall none succeed him for all generations forever.

25. In his priesthood, the Gentiles shall be multiplied in knowledge upon the earth, and enlightened through the grace of the Lord. In his priesthood shall sin come to an end, and the lawless shall cease to do evil.

26. He shall open the gates of paradise, and shall remove the threatening sword against Adam, and he shall give to the saints to eat from the tree of life, and the spirit of holiness shall be on them.

27. Satan shall be bound by him, and he shall give power to His children to tread upon the evil spirits.

28. The Lord shall rejoice in His children, and be well pleased in His beloved ones forever.

29. Then shall Abraham and Isaac and Jacob exult, and I will be glad, and all the saints shall clothe themselves with joy.

30. Now, my children, you have heard all; choose, therefore, for yourselves either the light or the darkness, either the law of the Lord or the works of Satan."

31. His sons answered him, saying, "Before the Lord we will walk according to His law."

32. Their father said to them, "The Lord is witness, and His angels are witnesses, and you are witnesses, and I am witness, concerning the word of your mouth."

33. His sons said to him: "We are witnesses."

34. So Levi ceased commanding his sons; and he stretched out his feet on the bed, and was gathered to his fathers, after he had lived a hundred and thirty-seven years.

35. They laid him in a coffin, and afterwards they buried him in Hebron, with Abraham, Isaac, and Jacob.

THE TESTAMENT OF JUDAH

The Fourth Son of Jacob and Leah

Chapter 1

1. THE copy of the words of Judah, what things he spoke to his sons before he died.

2. They gathered themselves together, therefore, and came to him, and he said to them: "Hearken, my children, to Judah your father.

3. I was the fourth son born to my father Jacob; and Leah my mother named me Judah, saying, 'I give thanks to the Lord, because He has given me a fourth son also.'

4. I was swift in my youth, and obedient to my father in everything.

5. I honored my mother and my mother's sister.

6. It came to pass, when I became a man, that my father blessed me, saying, 'You shall be a king, prospering in all things.'

7. The Lord showed me favor in all my works both in the field and in the house.

8. I know that I raced a hind and caught it, and prepared the meat for my father, and he ate it.

9. The roes I used to master in the chase, and overtake all that was in the plains.

10. A wild mare I overtook, and caught it and tamed it.

11. I slew a lion and plucked a kid out of its mouth.

12. I took a bear by its paw and hurled it down the cliff, and it was crushed.

13. I outran the wild boar, and seizing it as I ran, I tore it in sunder.

14. A leopard in Hebron leaped upon my dog, and I caught it by the tail, and hurled it on the rocks, and it was broken in two.

15. I found a wild ox feeding in the fields, and seizing it by the horns, and whirling it round and stunning it, I cast it from me and slew it.

16. When the two kings of the Canaanites came sheathed in armor against our flocks, and much people with them, single handedly I rushed upon the king of Hazor, and smote him on the greaves and dragged him down, and so I slew him.

17. The other, the king of Tappuah, as he sat upon his horse, I slew, and so I scattered all of his people.

18. Achor, the king, a man of giant stature, I found hurling javelins before and behind as he sat on horseback, and I took up a stone of sixty pounds weight and hurled it and smote his horse and killed it.

19. I fought with this other for two hours; and I clave his shield in twain, and I chopped off his feet and killed him.

20. As I was stripping off his breastplate, nine men his companions began to fight with me,

21. And I wound my garment on my hand; and I slung stones at them, and killed four of them, and the rest fled.

22. Jacob my father slew Beelesath, king of all the kings, a giant in strength, twelve cubits high.

23. Fear fell upon them, and they ceased warring against us.

24. Therefore my father was free from anxiety in the wars when I was with my brethren.

25. For he saw in a vision concerning me that an angel of might followed me everywhere, that I should not be overcome.

26. In the south there came upon us a greater war than that in Shechem; and I joined in battle array with my brethren and pursued a thousand men, and slew of them two hundred men and four kings.

27. I went up upon the wall, and I slew four mighty men.

28. So we captured Hazor, and we took all the spoil.

29. The next day, we departed to Aretan, a city strong and walled and inaccessible, threatening us with death.

30. But I and Gad approached on the east side of the city, and Reuben and Levi on the west.

31. They that were upon the wall, thinking that we were alone, were drawn down against us.

32. So my brothers secretly climbed up the wall on both sides by stakes, and entered the city, while the men knew it not.

33. We took it with the edge of the sword.

34. As for those who had taken refuge in the tower, we set fire to the tower and took both it and them.

35. As we were departing, the men of Tappuah seized our spoil, and seeing this, we fought with them.

36. We slew them all and recovered our spoil.

37. When I was at the waters of Kozeba, the men of Jobel came against us to battle.

38. We fought with them and routed them, and their allies from Shiloh we slew, and we did not leave them power to come in against us.

39. The men of Makir came upon us the fifth day, to seize our spoil, and we attacked them and overcame them in fierce battle, for there was a host of mighty men among them, and we slew them before they had gone up the ascent.

40. When we came to their city, their women rolled upon us stones from the brow of the hill on which the city stood.

41. I and Simeon hid ourselves behind the town, and seized upon the heights, and destroyed this city also.

42. The next day, it was told to us that the king of the city of Gaash with a mighty host was coming against us.

43. I, therefore, and Dan feigned ourselves to be Amorites, and as allies went into their city.

44. In the depth of night, our brethren came and we opened to them the gates; and we destroyed all the men and their substance, and we took for a prey all that was theirs, and their three walls we cast down.

45. We drew near to Thamna, where there was all the substance of the hostile kings.

46. Then being insulted by them, I was therefore angry, and I rushed against them to the summit; and they kept slinging against me stones and darts.

47. Had not Dan my brother aided me, they would have slain me.

48. We came upon them, therefore, with wrath, and they all fled; and passing by another way,

they fought my father, and he made peace with them.

49. We did them no hurt, and they became tributary to us, and we restored to them their spoil.

50. I built Thamna, and my father built Pabael.

51. I was twenty years old when this war befell, and the Canaanites feared me and my brethren.

52. I had much cattle, and I had for chief herdsman Iram the Adullamite,

53. And when I went to him, I saw Parsaba, king of Adullam, and he spoke to us, and he made us a feast; and when I was heated, he gave me his daughter Bathshua to wife.

54. She bare me Er and Onan and Shelah; and two of them the Lord smote, but Shelah lived, and his children are you.

Chapter 2

1. EIGHTEEN years my father abode in peace with his brother Esau, and his sons with us; and after that, we came from Mesopotamia, from Laban.

2. When eighteen years were fulfilled, in the fortieth year of my life, Esau, the brother of my father, came upon us with a mighty and strong people.

3. Jacob smote Esau with an arrow, and he was taken up wounded on Mount Seir, and as he went, he died at Anoniram.

4. We pursued after the sons of Esau.

5. Now they had a city with walls of iron and gates of brass; and we could not enter into it, and we encamped around and besieged it.

6. When they opened not to us in twenty days, I set up a ladder in the sight of all, and with my shield upon my head, I went up, sustaining the assault of stones, upwards of three talents weight; and I slew four of their mighty men.

7. Reuben and Gad slew six others.

8. Then they asked from us terms of peace; and having taken counsel with our father, we received them as tributaries.

9. They gave us five hundred cores of wheat, five hundred baths of oil, five hundred measures of wine, until the famine, when we went down into Egypt.

10. After these things, my son Er took to wife Tamar, from Mesopotamia, a daughter of Aram.

11. Now Er was wicked, and he was in need concerning Tamar, because she was not of the land of Canaan.

12. On the third night, an angel of the Lord smote him.

13. He had not known her according to the evil craftiness of his mother, for he did not wish to have children by her.

14. In the days of the wedding feast, I gave Onan to her in marriage; and he also in wickedness knew her not, though he spent with her a year.

15. When I threatened him, he went in to her, but he spilled the seed on the ground, according to the command of his mother, and he also died through wickedness.

16. I wished to give Shelah also to her, but his mother did not permit it; for she thought evil against Tamar, because she was not the daughters of Canaan, as she also herself was.

17. I knew that the race of the Canaanites was wicked, but the impulse of youth blinded my mind.

18. When I saw her pouring out wine, owing to the intoxication of wine, I was deceived, and I took her, although my father had not counselled it.

19. While I was away, she went and took for Shelah a wife from Canaan.

20. When I knew what she had done, I cursed her in the anguish of my soul.

21. She also died through her wickedness together with her sons.

22. After these things, while Tamar was a widow, she heard after two years that I was going up to shear my sheep, and she adorned herself in bridal array and sat in the city Enaim by the gate,

23. For it was a law of the Amorites that she who was about to marry should sit in fornication seven days by the gate.

24. Therefore, being drunk with wine, I did not recognize her; and her beauty deceived me, through the fashion of her adorning.

25. I turned aside to her, and said: 'Let me go in to you.'

26. She said: 'What will you give me?' I gave her my staff and my girdle and the diadem of my kingdom in pledge.

27. I went in to her, and she conceived.

28. Not knowing what I had done, I wished to slay her; but she privately sent my pledges, and put me to shame.

29. When I called her, I heard also the secret words which I spoke when lying with her in my drunkenness; and I could not slay her, because it was from the Lord.

30. For I said, lest it happened that she did it deceitfully, having received the pledge from another woman.

31. But I came not again near her while I lived, because I had done this abomination in all Israel.

32. Moreover, they who were in the city said there was no harlot in the gate, because she came from another place, and sat for a while in the gate.

33. I thought that no one knew that I had gone in to her.

34. After this, we came into Egypt to Joseph, because of the famine.

35. I was forty and six years old, and seventy and three years lived I in Egypt.

Chapter 3

1. NOW I command you, my children, hearken to Judah your father, and keep my sayings to perform all the ordinances of the Lord, and to obey the commands of God.

2. Walk not after your lusts, nor in the imaginations of your thoughts, in haughtiness of heart; and glory not in the deeds and strength of your youth, for this also is evil in the eyes of the Lord.

3. Since I also gloried that in wars, no comely woman's face ever enticed me, and reproved Reuben my brother concerning Bilhah, the wife of my father, the spirits of jealousy and of fornication arrayed themselves against me, until

I lay with Bathshua the Canaanite, and Tamar, who was espoused to my sons.

4. For I said to my father-in-law: 'I will take counsel with my father, and so will I take your daughter.'

5. He was unwilling, but he showed me a boundless store of gold in his daughter's behalf; for he was a king.

6. He adorned her with gold and pearls, and caused her to pour out wine for us at the feast with the beauty of women.

7. The wine turned aside my eyes, and pleasure blinded my heart.

8. I became enamored of her, and I lay with her, and I transgressed the commandment of the Lord and the commandment of my fathers, and I took her to wife.

9. The Lord rewarded me according to the imagination of my heart, inasmuch as I had no joy in her children.

10. Now, my children, I say to you, don't be drunk with wine; for wine turns the mind away from the truth, and inspires the passion of lust, and leads the eyes into error.

11. For the spirit of fornication has wine as a minister, to give pleasure to the mind; for these two also take away the mind of man.

12. For if a man drink wine to drunkenness, it disturbs the mind with filthy thoughts leading to fornication, and heats the body to carnal union; and if the occasion of the lust is present, he works the sin and is not ashamed.

13. Such is the inebriated man, my children; for he who is drunken reverences no man.

14. For it made me also to err, so that I was not ashamed of the multitude in the city, in that before the eyes of all, I turned aside to Tamar, and I worked a great sin, and I uncovered the covering of my sons' shame.

15. After I had drunk wine I reverenced not the commandment of God, and I took a woman of Canaan to wife.

16. For much discretion needs the man who drinks wine, my children; and herein is discretion in drinking wine, a man may drink so long as he preserves modesty.

17. But if he goes beyond this limit, the spirit of deceit attacks his mind, and it makes the drunkard to talk filthily, and to transgress and not to be ashamed, but even to glory in his shame, and to account himself honorable.

18. He that commits fornication is not aware when he suffers loss, and is not ashamed when put to dishonor.

19. For even though a man is a king and commits fornication, he is stripped of his kingship by becoming the slave of fornication, as I myself also suffered.

20. For I gave my staff, that is, the stay of my tribe, and my girdle, that is my power, and my diadem, that is the glory of my kingdom.

21. Indeed, I repented of these things, and wine and flesh I did not eat until my old age, nor did I have any joy.

22. The angel of God showed me that forever will women bear rule over king and beggar alike.

23. From the king, they take away his glory, and from the valiant man, his might, and from the beggar, even that little which is the stay of his poverty.

24. Observe, therefore, my children, the right limit in wine; for there are in it four evil spirits: of lust, of hot desire, of recklessness, of filthy lucre.

25. If you drink wine in gladness, be modest in the fear of God.

26. For if in your gladness the fear of God departs, then drunkenness arises and shamelessness steals in.

27. But if you would live soberly, do not touch wine at all, lest you sin in words of outrage, and in fighting and slander, and transgressions of the commandments of God, and you perish before your time.

28. Moreover, wine reveals the mysteries of God and men, even as I also revealed the commandments of God and the mysteries of Jacob my father to the Canaanitish woman Bathshua, which God bade me not to reveal.

29. Wine is a cause both of war and confusion.

30. Now, I command you, my children, not to love money, nor to gaze upon the beauty of women; because for the sake of money and beauty, I was led astray to Bathshua the Canaanite.

31. For I know that because of these two things shall my race fall into wickedness.

32. For even wise men among my sons shall they mar, and shall cause the kingdom of Judah to be diminished, which the Lord gave me because of my obedience to my father.

33. For I never caused grief to Jacob, my father; for all things whatsoever he commanded, I did.

34. Isaac, the father of my father, blessed me to be king in Israel, and Jacob further blessed me in like manner.

35. I know that from me shall the kingdom be established.

36. I know what evils you will do in the last days.

37. Beware, therefore, my children, of fornication and the love of money, and hearken to Judah your father.

38. For these things draw you away from the law of God, and blind the inclination of the soul, and teach arrogance, and suffer not a man to have compassion upon his neighbor.

39. They rob his soul of all goodness, and oppress him with toils and troubles, and drive away sleep from him, and devour his flesh.

40. He hinders the sacrifices of God; and he remembers not the blessing of God, he hearkens not to a prophet when he speaks, and he resents the words of godliness.

41. For he is a slave to two contrary passions, and cannot obey God, because they have blinded his soul, and he walks in the day as in the night.

42. My children, the love of money leads to idolatry; because, when led astray through money, men name as gods those who are not gods, and it causes him who has it to fall into madness.

43. For the sake of money, I lost my children, and I had no repentance, and if my humiliation and the prayers of my father had not been accepted, I should have died childless.

44. But the God of my fathers had mercy on me, because I did it in ignorance.

45. The prince of deceit blinded me, and I sinned as a man and as flesh, being corrupted through sins; and I learned my own weakness while thinking myself invincible.

46. Know, therefore, my children, that two spirits wait upon man: the spirit of truth and the spirit of deceit.

47. In the midst is the spirit of understanding of the mind, to which it belongs to turn a man where so ever it will.

48. The works of truth and the works of deceit are written upon the hearts of men, and each one of them the Lord knows.

49. There is no time at which the works of men can be hid; for on the heart itself have they been written down before the Lord.

50. The spirit of truth testifies all things, and accuses all; and the sinner is burned up by his own heart, and cannot raise his face to the judge.

Chapter 4

1. NOW, my children, I command you, love Levi, that you may abide, and exalt not yourselves against him, lest you be utterly destroyed.

2. For to me, the Lord gave the kingdom, and to him the priesthood, and He set the kingdom beneath the priesthood.

3. To me He gave the things upon the earth; to him the things in the heavens.

4. As the heaven is higher than the earth, so is the priesthood of God higher than the earthly kingdom, unless it falls away through sin from the Lord and is dominated by the earthly kingdom.

5. For the angel of the Lord said to me: 'The Lord chose Levi rather than you, to draw near to Him, and to eat of His table and to offer Him the first-fruits of the choice things of the sons of Israel; but you shall be king of Jacob;

6. And you shall be among them as the sea.

7. For as, on the sea, just and unjust are tossed about, some taken into captivity while some are enriched, so also shall every race of men be in you; some shall be impoverished, being taken captive, and others grow rich by plundering the possessions of others.

8. For the kings shall be as sea-monsters.

9. They shall swallow men like fish, the sons and daughters of freemen shall they enslave; houses, lands, flocks, money shall they plunder;

10. And with the flesh of many shall they wrongfully feed the ravens and the cranes; and they shall advance in evil, in covetousness uplifted, and there shall be false prophets like tempest, and they shall persecute all righteous men.

11. The Lord shall bring upon them divisions one against another.

12. There shall be continual wars in Israel; and among men of another race shall my kingdom

be brought to an end, until the salvation of Israel shall come.

13. Until the appearing of the God of righteousness, that Jacob, and all the Gentiles may rest in peace.

14. He shall guard the might of my kingdom forever; for the Lord made aware to me with an oath that He would not destroy the kingdom from my seed forever.

15. Now I have much grief, my children, because of your lewdness and witchcrafts and idolatries which you shall practice against the kingdom, following them that have familiar spirits, diviners, and demons of error.

16. You shall make your daughters singing girls and harlots, and you shall mingle in the abominations of the Gentiles.

17. For which things' sake the Lord shall bring upon you famine and pestilence, death and the sword, beleaguering by enemies, and condemnations from friends, the slaughter of

children, the rape of wives, the plundering of possessions, the burning of the temple of God, the laying waste of the land, the enslavement of yourselves among the Gentiles.

18. They shall make some of you eunuchs for their wives,

19. Until the Lord visits you, when with perfect heart you repent and walk in all His commandments, and He bring you up from captivity among the Gentiles.

20. After these things shall a star arise to you from Jacob in peace,

21. And a man shall arise from my seed, like the sun of righteousness,

22. Walking with the sons of men in meekness and righteousness;

23. And no sin shall be found in him.

24. The heavens shall be opened to him, to pour out the spirit, even the blessing of the Holy

Father; and He shall pour out the spirit of grace upon you;

25. And you shall be to Him sons in truth, and you shall walk in His commandments first and last.

26. Then shall the scepter of my kingdom shine forth; and from your root shall arise a stem; and from it shall grow a rod of righteousness to the Gentiles, to judge and to save all that call upon the Lord.

27. And after these things shall Abraham and Isaac and Jacob arise to life; and I and my brethren shall be chiefs of the tribes of Israel,

28. Levi first, I the second, Joseph third, Benjamin fourth, Simeon fifth, Issachar sixth, and so all in order.

29. The Lord blessed Levi, and the Angel of the Presence, me; the powers of glory, Simeon; the heaven, Reuben; the earth, Issachar; the sea, Zebulun; the mountains, Joseph; the tabernacle,

Benjamin; the luminaries, Dan; Eden, Naphtali; the sun, Gad; the moon, Asher.

30. You shall be the people of the Lord, and have one tongue; and there shall be there no spirit of deceit of Satan, for he shall be cast into the fire forever.

31. They who have died in grief shall arise in joy, and they who were poor for the Lord's sake shall be made rich, and they who are put to death for the Lord's sake shall awake to life.

32. The hearts of Jacob shall run in joyfulness, and the eagles of Israel shall fly in gladness; and all the people shall glorify the Lord forever.

33. Observe, therefore, my children, all the law of the Lord, for there is hope for all those who hold fast to His ways."

34. He said to them: "Behold, I die before your eyes this day, a hundred and nineteen years old.

35. Let no one bury me in costly apparel, nor tear open my bowels, for this shall they who are kings do; and carry me up to Hebron with you."

36. Judah, when he had said these things, fell asleep; and his sons did according to all whatsoever he commanded them, and they buried him in Hebron, with his fathers.

THE TESTAMENT OF ISSACHAR

The Fifth Son of Jacob and Leah

Chapter 1

1. THE copy of the words of Issachar.

2. For he called his sons and said to them: "Hearken, my children, to Issachar your father; give ear to the words of him who is beloved of the Lord.

3. I was born the fifth son to Jacob, by way of hire for the mandrakes.

4. For Reuben my brother brought in mandrakes from the field, and Rachel met him and took them,

5. And Reuben wept, and at his voice Leah my mother came forth.

6. Now these mandrakes were sweet-smelling apples which were produced in the land of Haran below a ravine of water.

7. Rachel said: 'I will not give them to you, but they shall be to me instead of children.

8. For the Lord has despised me, and I have not borne children to Jacob.'

9. Now there were two apples, and Leah said to Rachel: 'Let it suffice that you have taken my husband, will you take these also?'

10. Rachel said to her: 'You shall have Jacob this night for the mandrakes of your son.'

11. Leah said to her: 'Jacob is mine, for I am the wife of his youth.'

12. But Rachel said: 'Boast not, and vaunt not yourself; for he espoused me before you, and for my sake, he served our father fourteen years.

13. Had not craft increased on the earth and the wickedness of men prospered, you would not now see the face of Jacob.

14. For you are not his wife, but in craft were taken to him in my stead.

15. My father deceived me and removed me on that night, and did not suffer Jacob to see me; for had I been there, this would not have happened to him.

16. Nevertheless, for the mandrakes, I am hiring Jacob to you for one night.'

17. Jacob knew Leah, and she conceived and bare me, and on account of the hire, I was called Issachar.

18. Then appeared to Jacob an angel of the Lord, saying: 'Two children shall Rachel bear, inasmuch as she has refused company with her husband, and has chosen abstinence.'

19. Had not Leah my mother paid the two apples for the sake of his company, she would have borne eight sons; for this reason she bare six, and Rachel bare the two; for on account of the mandrakes the Lord visited her.

20. For He knew that for the sake of children, she wished to company with Jacob, and not for lust of pleasure.

21. For on the morrow also she again gave up Jacob.

22. Because of the mandrakes, therefore, the Lord hearkened to Rachel.

23. For though she desired them, she ate them not, but offered them in the house of the Lord, presenting them to the priest of the Most High who was at that time.

24. When, therefore, I grew up, my children, I walked in uprightness of heart, and I became a husbandman for my father and my brethren, and I brought in fruits from the field according to their season.

25. My father blessed me, for he saw that I walked in rectitude before him.

26. I was not a busybody in my doings, nor envious and malicious against my neighbor.

27. I never slandered anyone, nor did I censure the life of any man, walking as I did in singleness of eye.

28. Therefore, when I was thirty-five years old, I took to myself a wife, for my labor wore away my strength, and I never thought upon pleasure with women; but owing to my toil, sleep overcame me.

29. My father always rejoiced in my rectitude, because I offered through the priest to the Lord all first-fruits, then to my father also.

30. The Lord increased ten thousand fold His benefits in my hands; and also Jacob, my father, knew that God aided my singleness.

31. For on all the poor and oppressed I bestowed the good things of the earth in the singleness of my heart.

32. Now, hearken to me, my children, and walk in singleness of your heart, for I have seen in it all that is well-pleasing to the Lord.

33. The single-minded man covets not gold, he overreaches not his neighbor, he longs not after manifold dainties, he delights not in varied apparel.

34. He does not desire to live a long life, but only waits for the will of God.

35. The spirits of deceit have no power against him, for he looks not on the beauty of women, lest he should pollute his mind with corruption.

36. There is no envy in his thoughts, no malicious person makes his soul to pine away, nor worry with insatiable desire in his mind.

37. For he walks in singleness of soul, and beholds all things in uprightness of heart, shunning eyes made evil through the error of the world, lest he should see the perversion of any of the commandments of the Lord.

38. Keep, therefore, my children, the law of God, and get singleness, and walk in guilelessness, not playing the busybody with the business of your neighbor, but love the Lord and your neighbor, have compassion on the poor and weak.

39. Bow down your back to husbandry, and toil in labors in all manner of husbandry, offering gifts to the Lord with thanksgiving.

40. For with the first-fruits of the earth will the Lord bless you, even as He blessed all the saints from Abel even until now.

41. For no other portion is given to you than of the fatness of the earth, whose fruits are raised by toil.

42. For our father Jacob blessed me with blessings of the earth and of first-fruits,

43. And Levi and Judah were glorified by the Lord even among the sons of Jacob; for the Lord gave them an inheritance, and to Levi He gave the priesthood, and to Judah the kingdom.

44. And do therefore obey them, and walk in the singleness of your father; for to Gad has it been given to destroy the troops that are coming upon Israel.

Chapter 2

1. KNOW therefore, my children, that in the last times, your sons will forsake singleness, and will cleave to insatiable desire.

2. Leaving guilelessness, they will draw near to malice; and forsaking the commandments of the Lord, they will cleave to Satan.

3. Leaving husbandry, they will follow after their own wicked devices, and they shall be dispersed among the Gentiles, and shall serve their enemies.

4. Therefore, give these commands to your children, that, if they sin, they may the more quickly return to the Lord; for He is merciful, and will deliver them, even to bring them back into their land.

5. As you see, I am a hundred and twenty-six years old and am not conscious of committing any sin.

6. Except my wife, I have not known any woman. I never committed fornication by the uplifting of my eyes.

7. I drank not wine, to be led astray thereby;

8. I coveted not any desirable thing that was my neighbor's.

9. Guile arose not in my heart;

10. A lie passed not through my lips.

11. If any man were in distress I joined my sighs with his,

12. And I shared my bread with the poor.

13. I wrought godliness; all my days I kept truth.

14. I loved the Lord, and likewise also every man with all of my heart.

15. So you also do these things, my children, and every spirit of Satan shall flee from you, and no deed of wicked men shall rule over you;

16. And every wild beast shall you subdue, since you have with you the God of heaven and earth and walk with men in singleness of heart."

17. Having said these things, he commanded his sons that they should carry him up to Hebron, and bury him there in the cave with his fathers.

18. And he stretched out his feet and died, at a good old age, with every limb sound, and with strength unabated, he slept the eternal sleep.

THE TESTAMENT OF ZEBULUN

The Sixth Son of Jacob and Leah

Chapter 1

1. THE copy of the words of Zebulun, which he enjoined on his sons before he died in the hundred and fourteenth year of his life, two years after the death of Joseph.

2. He said to them: "Hearken to me, you sons of Zebulun, and attend to the words of your father.

3. I, Zebulun, was born a good gift to my parents.

4. For when I was born, my father was increased very exceedingly, both in flocks and herds, when with the streaked rods he had his portion.

5. I am not conscious that I have sinned all my days, save in thought.

6. Nor yet do I remember that I have done any iniquity, except the sin of ignorance which I

committed against Joseph; for I covenanted with my brethren not to tell my father what had been done.

7. But I wept in secret many days on account of Joseph, for I feared my brethren, because they had all agreed that if anyone should declare the secret, he should be slain.

8. But when they wished to kill him, I adjured them much with tears not to be guilty of this sin.

9. For Simeon and Gad came against Joseph to kill him, and he said to them with tears: 'Pity me, my brethren, have mercy upon the bowels of Jacob our father and lay not upon me your hands to shed innocent blood, for I have not sinned against you.

10. And if indeed I have sinned, with chastening chastise me, my brethren, but lay not upon me your hand, for the sake of Jacob our father.'

11. As he spoke these words, wailing as he did so, I was unable to bear his lamentations, and began to weep, and my liver was poured out,

and all the substance of my bowels was loosened.

12. I wept with Joseph and my heart sounded, and the joints of my body trembled, and I was not able to stand.

13. When Joseph saw me weeping with him, and them coming against him to slay him, he fled behind me, beseeching them.

14. But meanwhile Reuben arose and said: 'Come, my brethren, let us not slay him, but let us cast him into one of these dry pits, which our fathers dug and found no water.'

15. For for this cause the Lord forbade that water should rise up in them in order that Joseph should be preserved.

16. They did so, until they sold him to the Ishmaelites.

17. For in his price, I had no share, my children.

18. But Simeon and Gad and six others of our brethren took the price of Joseph, and they

bought sandals for themselves, and for their wives, and for their children, saying:

19. 'We will not eat of it, for it is the price of our brother's blood, but we will assuredly tread it under foot, because he said that he would be king over us, and so let us see what will become of his dreams.'

20. Therefore it is written in the writing of the law of Moses, that whosoever will not raise up seed to his brother, his sandal should be unloosed, and they should spit in his face.

21. The brethren of Joseph wished not that their brother should live, and the Lord loosed from them the sandal which they wore against Joseph their brother.

22. For when they came into Egypt, they were unloosed by the servants of Joseph outside the gate, and so they made homage to Joseph after the fashion of King Pharaoh.

23. Not only did they make homage to him, but were spit upon also, falling down before him,

and so they were put to shame before the Egyptians.

24. For after this, the Egyptians heard all the evils that they had done to Joseph.

25. After he was sold, my brothers sat down to eat and drink.

26. But I, through pity for Joseph, did not eat, but I watched the pit, since Judah feared lest Simeon, Dan, and Gad should rush off and slay him.

27. But when they saw that I did not eat, they set me to watch him, until he was sold to the Ishmaelites.

28. When Reuben came and heard that while he was away Joseph had been sold, he rent his garments, and mourning, he said:

29. 'How shall I look on the face of my father Jacob? He took the money and ran after the merchants but as he failed to find them he returned grieving.

30. But the merchants had left the broad road and marched through the Troglodytes by a short cut.

31. But Reuben was grieved, and ate no food that day.

32. Dan therefore came to him and said: 'Weep not, neither grieve; for we have found what we can say to our father Jacob.

33. Let us slay a kid of the goats and dip in it the coat of Joseph; and let us send it to Jacob, saying: Do you know if this the coat of your son?'

34. And they did so. They stripped off from Joseph his coat when they were selling him, and put upon him the garment of a slave.

35. Now Simeon took the coat and would not give it up, for he wished to rend it with his sword, as he was angry that Joseph lived and that he had not slain him.

36. Then we all rose up and said to him: 'If you do not give up the coat, we will say to our father that you alone did this evil thing in Israel,'

37. And so he gave it to them, and they did even as Dan had said.

Chapter 2

1. NOW children, I adjure you to keep the commands of the Lord, and to show mercy to your neighbors, and to have compassion towards all, not towards men only, but also towards beasts.

2. For all of these things sake, the Lord blessed me, and when all my brethren were sick, I escaped without sickness, for the Lord knows the purposes of each.

3. Have, therefore, compassion in your hearts, my children, because even as a man does to his neighbor, even so also will the Lord do to him.

4. For the sons of my brethren were sickly and were dying on account of Joseph, because they showed not mercy in their hearts; but my sons were preserved without sickness, as you know.

5. When I was in the land of Canaan, by the sea-coast, I made a catch of fish for Jacob my father;

and when many were choked in the sea, I continued unhurt.

6. I was the first to make a boat to sail upon the sea, for the Lord gave me understanding and wisdom to do it.

7. I let down a rudder behind it, and I stretched a sail upon another upright piece of wood in the midst,

8. And I sailed therein along the shores, catching fish for the house of my father until we came to Egypt.

9. Through compassion I shared my catch with every stranger.

10. If a man were a stranger or sick or aged, I boiled the fish and dressed them well, and I offered them to all men, as every man had need, grieving with and having compassion upon them.

11. Wherefore also the Lord satisfied me with abundance of fish when catching fish; for he that shares with his neighbor receives manifold more from the Lord.

12. For five years I caught fish and gave to every man whom I saw, and sufficed for all the house of my father.

13. In the summer, I caught fish, and in the winter, I kept sheep with my brethren.

14. Now I will declare to you what I did.

15. I saw a man in distress through nakedness in wintertime, and I had compassion on him, and I stole away a garment secretly from my father's house, and I gave it to him who was in distress.

16. Do you, therefore, my children, from that which God bestows upon you, show compassion and mercy without hesitation to all men, and give to every man with a good heart.

17. If you have not the wherewithal to give to him that needs, have compassion for him in bowels of mercy.

18. I know that my hand found not the wherewithal to give to him that needed, and I walked with him weeping for seven furlongs, and my bowels yearned towards him in compassion.

19. Have also, my children, compassion towards every man with mercy, that the Lord also may have compassion and mercy upon you.

20. Because also in the last days, God will send His compassion on the earth, and wheresoever He finds bowels of mercy, He dwells in him.

21. For in the degree in which a man has compassion upon his neighbors, in the same degree has the Lord also upon him.

22. When we went down into Egypt, Joseph bore no malice against us.

23. So, you have no malice toward others either, my children, and approve yourselves without malice, and love one another; and do not set down in account, each one of you, evil against his brother.

24. For this breaks unity and divides all kindred and troubles the soul and wears away the countenance.

25. Observe, therefore, the waters, and know when they flow together, they sweep along stones, trees, earth, and other things.

26. But if they are divided into many streams, the earth swallows them up, and they vanish away.

27. So shall you also be, if you are divided. Be not, therefore, divided into two heads, for everything which the Lord made has but one head, and two shoulders, two hands, two feet, and all the remaining members.

28. For I have learned in the writing of my fathers, that you shall be divided in Israel, and you shall follow two kings, and shall work every abomination.

29. Your enemies shall lead you captive, and you shall be evil treated among the Gentiles, with many infirmities and tribulations.

30. After these things, you shall remember the Lord and repent, and He shall have mercy upon you, for He is merciful and compassionate.

31. He sets not down in account evil against the sons of men, because they are flesh, and are deceived through their own wicked deeds.

32. After these things shall there arise unto you the Lord Himself, the light of righteousness, and you shall return to your land,

33. And you shall see Him in Jerusalem, for His name's sake,

34. And again, through the wickedness of your works shall you provoke Him to anger,

35. And you shall be cast away by Him unto the time of consummation.

36. Now, my children, grieve not that I am dying, nor be cast down in that I am coming to my end.

37. For I shall rise again in the midst of you, as a ruler in the midst of his sons; and I shall rejoice

in the midst of my tribe, as many as shall keep the law of the Lord, and the commandments of Zebulun their father.

38. But upon the ungodly shall the Lord bring eternal fire, and destroy them throughout all generations.

39. But I am now hastening away to my rest, as did also my fathers.

40. But fear the Lord our God with all of your strength all the days of your life."

41. When he had said these things, he fell asleep at a good old age.

42. His sons laid him in a wooden coffin, and afterwards, they carried him up and buried him in Hebron with his fathers.

THE TESTAMENT OF DAN

The Seventh Son of Jacob and Bilhah

Chapter 1

1. THE copy of the words of Dan, which he spoke to his sons in his last days, in the hundred and twenty-fifth year of his life.

2. For he called together his I family, and he said: "Hearken to my words, sons of Dan; and give heed to the words of your father.

3. I have proved in my heart, and in my whole life, that truth with just dealing is good and well pleasing to God, and that lying and anger are evil, because they teach man all wickedness.

4. I confess this day to you, my children, that in my heart I resolved on the death of Joseph my brother, the true and good man. . .

5. I rejoiced that he was sold, because his father loved him more than us.

6. For the spirit of jealousy and vainglory said to me: 'You also are his son.'

7. One of the spirits of Satan stirred me up, saying: 'Take this sword, and with it slay Joseph, then shall your father love you after Joseph is dead.'

8. Now this is the spirit of anger that persuaded me to crush Joseph as a leopard crushes a kid.

9. But the God of my fathers did not suffer him to fall into my hands, so that I should find him alone and slay him, and cause a second tribe to be destroyed in Israel.

10. Now, my children, I am dying, and I tell you of a truth, that unless you keep yourselves from the spirit of lying and of anger, and love truth and longsuffering, you shall perish.

11. For anger is blindness, and does not suffer one to see the face of any man with truth.

12. For though it is a father or a mother, he behaves towards them as enemies; though it is a brother, he knows him not; though it be a

prophet of the Lord, he disobeys him; though a righteous man, he regards him not; though a friend, he does not acknowledge him.

13. For the spirit of anger encompasses him with the net of deceit, and blinds his eyes, and through lying darkens his mind, and gives him its own peculiar vision.

14. With what does it encompass his eyes? With hatred of heart, so as to be envious of his brother.

15. For anger is an evil thing, my children, for it troubles even the soul itself.

16. The body of the angry man, it makes its own, and over his soul it gets the mastery, and it bestows upon the body power that it may work all iniquity.

17. When the body does all these things, the soul justifies what has been done, since it sees wrongly.

18. Therefore, he that is wrathful, if he is a mighty man, has a threefold power in his anger:

he has servants to help him; and a second by his wealth, whereby he persuades and overcomes wrongfully; and thirdly, having his own natural, physical power, he works violence and evil.

19. Though the wrathful man may be weak, yet has a power twofold, of that which is by nature, for wrath ever aides even the weak in lawlessness.

20. This spirit goes always with lying at the right hand of Satan, that with cruelty and lying, his works may be done.

21. Understand, therefore, the power of wrath, that it is vain.

22. For it first of all gives provocation by word; then by deeds, it strengthens him who is angry, and with sharp losses, it disturbs his mind, and so stirs up with great wrath his soul.

23. Therefore, when anyone speaks against you, don't be moved to anger, and if any man praises you as holy men, do not be uplifted; do not be moved either to delight or to disgust.

24. For first it pleases the hearing, and so makes the mind keen to perceive the grounds for provocation; and then being enraged, he thinks that he is justly angry.

25. If you fall into any loss or ruin, my children, don't be afflicted; for this very spirit makes a man desire that which is perishable, in order that he may be enraged through the affliction.

26. If you suffer loss voluntarily, or involuntarily, don't be vexed; for from vexation arises wrath with lying.

27. Moreover, a twofold mischief is wrath with lying; and they assist one another in order to disturb the heart; and when the soul is continually disturbed, the Lord departs from it, and Satan rules over it.

Chapter 2

1. OBSERVE, therefore, my children, the commandments of the Lord, and keep His law; depart from wrath, and hate lying, that the Lord may dwell among you, and Satan may flee from you.

2. Speak truth each one with his neighbor. So shall you not fall into wrath and confusion; but you shall be in peace, having the God of peace, so shall no war prevail over you.

3. Love the Lord throughout all of your life, and one another with a true heart.

4. I know that in the last days, you shall depart from the Lord, and you shall provoke Levi to anger, and fight against Judah; but you shall not prevail against them, for an angel of the Lord shall guide them both; for by them shall Israel stand.

5. When you depart from the Lord, you shall walk in all evil and work the abominations of the Gentiles, going a-whoring after women of

the lawless ones, while with all wickedness the spirits of wickedness work in you.

6. For I have read in the book of Enoch, the righteous, that your prince is Satan, and that all the spirits of wickedness and pride will conspire to attend constantly on the sons of Levi, to cause them to sin before the Lord.

7. My sons will draw near to Levi and sin with them in all things; and the sons of Judah will be covetous, plundering other men's goods like lions.

8. Therefore shall you be led away with them into captivity, and there shall you receive all the plagues of Egypt, and all the evils of the Gentiles.

9. So when you return to the Lord, you shall obtain mercy, and He shall bring you into His sanctuary, and He shall give you peace.

10. There shall arise unto you from the tribe of Judah and of Levi the salvation of the Lord; and he shall make war against Satan, and

11. Execute an everlasting vengeance on our enemies; and the captivity, shall he take from Satan, the souls of the saints, and turn disobedient hearts to the Lord, and give to them that call upon him eternal peace.

12. The saints shall rest in Eden, and in the New Jerusalem shall the righteous rejoice, and it shall be to the glory of God forever.

13. No longer shall Jerusalem endure desolation, nor Israel be led captive; for the Lord shall be in the midst of it [living among men], and the Holy One of Israel shall reign over it in humility and in poverty; and he who believes on Him shall reign among men in truth.

14. Now, fear the Lord, my children, and beware of Satan and his spirits.

15. Draw near to God and to the angel that intercedes for you, for he is a mediator between God and man, and for the peace of Israel he shall stand up against the kingdom of the enemy.

16. Therefore is the enemy eager to destroy all that call upon the Lord.

17. For he knows that upon the day on which Israel shall repent, the kingdom of the enemy shall be brought to an end.

18. For the very angel of peace shall strengthen Israel, that it fall not into the extremity of evil.

19. It shall be in the time of the lawlessness of Israel, that the Lord will not depart from them, but will transform them into a nation that does His will, for none of the angels will be equal to him.

20. His name shall be in every place in Israel, and among the Gentiles.

21. Keep, therefore, yourselves, my children, from every evil work, and cast away wrath and all lying, and love truth and long-suffering.

22. The things which you have heard from your father, do also impart to your children that the Savior of the Gentiles may receive you; for he is

true and long-suffering, meek and lowly, and teaches by his works the law of God.

23. Depart, therefore, from all unrighteousness, and cleave to the righteousness of God, and your race will be saved forever.

24. Bury me near my fathers."

25. And when he had said these things, he kissed them, and fell asleep at a good old age.

26. His sons buried him, and after that, they carried up his bones and placed them near Abraham, and Isaac, and Jacob.

27. Nevertheless, Dan prophesied to them that they would forget their God, and would be alienated from the land of their inheritance and from the race of Israel and from the family of their seed.

THE TESTAMENT OF NAPHTALI

The Eighth Son of Jacob and Bilhah

Chapter 1

1. THE copy of the testament of Naphtali, which he ordained at the time of his death in the hundred and thirtieth year of his life.

2. When his sons were gathered together in the seventh month, on the first day of the month, while still in good health, he made them a feast of food and wine.

3. After he was awake in the morning, he said to them, I am dying; and they did not believe him.

4. As he glorified the Lord, he grew strong and said that after the feast, he should die.

5. He began then to say: "Hear, my children, sons of Naphtali, hear the words of your father.

6. I was born from Bilhah, and because Rachel dealt craftily, and gave Bilhah in place of herself

to Jacob, and she conceived and bare me upon Rachel's knees, therefore she called my name Naphtali.

7. For Rachel loved me very much because I was born upon her lap; and when I was still young, she liked to kiss me, and say: 'May I have a brother of yours from my own womb, like you.'

8. Joseph was like me in all things, according to the prayers of Rachel.

9. Now my mother was Bilhah, daughter of Rotheus, the brother of Deborah, Rebecca's nurse, who was born on one and the self-same day with Rachel.

10. Rotheus was of the family of Abraham, a Chaldean, God-fearing, free-born, and noble.

11. He was taken captive and was bought by Laban; and he gave him Euna his handmaid to wife, and she bore a daughter, and called her name Zilpah, after the name of the village in which he had been taken captive.

12. Next she bore Bilhah, saying: 'My daughter hastens after what is new,' for immediately after she was born, she seized the breast and hastened to suck it.

13. I was swift on my feet like the deer, and my father Jacob appointed me for all messages, and as a deer did he give me his blessing.

14. For as the potter knows the vessel, and how much it can contain, and he brings clay accordingly; and so the Lord also makes the body after the likeness of the spirit, and according to the capacity of the body does He implant the spirit.

15. The one does not fall short of the other by a third part of a hair; for by weight and measure, by this rule was all of the creation made.

16. As the potter knows the use of each vessel, what it is meant for, so also does the Lord know the body, how far it will persist in goodness, and when it begins in evil.

17. For there is no inclination or thought which the Lord knows not, for He created every man after His own image.

18. For as a man's strength, so also is his work; as his eye, so also is his sleep; as his soul, so also is his word, either in the law of the Lord or in the law of Satan.

19. As there is a division between light and darkness, between seeing and hearing, so also is there a division between man and man, and between woman and woman; and it is not to be said that the one is like the other either in face or in mind.

20. For God made all things good in their order, the five senses in the head, and He joined the neck to the head, adding to it the hair also for comeliness and glory, then the heart for understanding, the belly for excrement, and the stomach for grinding, the windpipe for taking in the breath, the liver for wrath, the gall for bitterness, the spleen for laughter, the reins for prudence, the muscles of the loins for power, the

lungs for drawing in, the loins for strength, and so forth.

21. So then, my children, let all of your works be done in order, with good intent, in the fear of God, and do nothing disorderly in scorn or out of its due season.

22. For if you bid the eye to hear, it cannot; so neither while you are in darkness can you do the works of light.

23. Do not, therefore, be eager to corrupt your doings through covetousness or with vain words to beguile your souls; because if you keep silence in purity of heart, you shall understand how to hold fast to the will of God, and to cast away the will of Satan.

24. Sun and moon and stars change not their order; so you also do not change the law of God in the disorderliness of your doings.

25. The Gentiles went astray and forsook the Lord, and they changed their order and obeyed idols of wood and stone, spirits of deceit.

26. But you shall not be so, my children, recognizing in the firmament, in the earth, and in the sea, and in all created things, the Lord who made all things, that you become not as Sodom, which changed the order of nature.

27. In like manner, the Watchers also changed the order of their nature, whom the Lord cursed at the flood, on whose account He made the earth without inhabitants and fruitless.

28. These things I say to you, my children, for I have read in the writing of Enoch that you yourselves also shall depart from the Lord, walking according to all the lawlessness of the Gentiles, and you shall do according to all the wickedness of Sodom.

29. The Lord shall bring captivity upon you, and there shall you serve your enemies, and you shall be bowed down with every affliction and tribulation, until the Lord has consumed you all.

30. After you have become diminished and made few, you will return and acknowledge the Lord your God; and He shall bring you back

into your land, according to His abundant mercy.

31. It shall be that after that, when they come into the land of their fathers, they shall again forget the Lord and become ungodly.

32. The Lord shall scatter them upon the face of all the earth, until the compassion of the Lord shall come, a man working righteousness and working mercy to all them that are afar off, and to them that are near.

Chapter 2

1. FOR in the fortieth year of my life, I saw a vision on the Mount of Olives, on the east of Jerusalem, that the sun and the moon were standing still.

2. Isaac, the father of my father, said to us; 'Run and lay hold of them, each one according to his strength; and to him that seizes them will the sun and moon belong.'

3. We all of us ran together, and Levi laid hold of the sun, and Judah outstripped the others and seized the moon, and they were both of them lifted up with them.

4. When Levi became as a sun, a certain young man gave to him twelve branches of palm; and Judah was bright as the moon, and under their feet were twelve rays.

5. The two, Levi and Judah, ran and laid hold of them.

6. Then there was a bull upon the earth, with two great horns, with eagles wings on its back; and we wished to seize him, but could not.

7. But Joseph came and seized him, and ascended up with him on high.

8. I saw, for I was there, and a holy writing appeared to us, saying: 'Assyrians, Medes, Persians, Chaldeans, Syrians, shall possess in captivity the twelve tribes of Israel.'

9. Again, after seven days, I saw our father Jacob standing by the sea of Jamnia, and we were with him.

10. There came a ship sailing by, without sailors or pilot; and there was written upon the ship, The Ship of Jacob.

11. Our father said to us: 'Come, let us embark on our ship.'

12. When he had gone on board, there arose a vehement storm, and a mighty tempest of wind;

and our father, who was holding the helm, departed from us.

13. We, being lost with the tempest, were borne along over the sea; and the ship was filled with water, and was pounded by mighty waves, until it was broken up.

14. Joseph fled away upon a little boat, and we were all divided upon nine planks, and Levi and Judah were together.

15. We were all scattered unto the ends of the earth.

16. Then Levi, girt about with sackcloth, prayed for us all to the Lord.

17. When the storm ceased, the ship reached the land as it were in peace.

18. Our father came, and we all rejoiced with one accord.

19. These two dreams I told to my father; and he said to me: 'These things must be fulfilled in their season, after Israel has endured many things.'

20. Then my father said to me: 'I believe God that Joseph lives, for I see always that the Lord numbers him with you.'

21. He said, weeping: 'Ah me, my son Joseph, you live, though I behold you not, and you see not Jacob that begat you.

22. He caused me also, therefore, to weep by these words, and I burned in my heart to declare

that Joseph had been sold, but I feared my brethren.

23. My children, I have shown to you the last times, how everything shall come to pass in Israel.

24. Do you also, therefore, charge your children that they be united to Levi and to Judah; for through them shall salvation arise unto Israel, and in them shall Jacob be blessed.

25. For through their tribes shall God appear, dwelling among men on earth, to save the race of Israel, and to gather together the righteous from among the Gentiles.

26. If you work that which is good, my children, both men and angels shall bless you; and God shall be glorified among the Gentiles through you, and the devil shall flee from you, and the wild beasts shall fear you, and the Lord shall love you, and the angels shall cleave to you.

27. As a man who has trained a child well is kept in kindly remembrance; so also for a good work, there is a good remembrance before God.

28. But he that does not do that which is good, both angels and men shall curse, and God shall be dishonored among the Gentiles through him, and the devil shall make him as his own peculiar instrument, and every wild beast shall master him, and the Lord shall hate him.

29. For the commandments of the law are twofold, and through prudence must they be fulfilled.

30. For there is a season for a man to embrace his wife, and a season to abstain for his prayer.

31. So then, there are two commandments; and unless they are done in due order, they bring very great sin upon men.

32. So also is it with the other commandments.

33. Be wise in God, my children, and prudent, understanding the order of His commandments,

and the laws of every word, that the Lord may love you."

34. When he had charged them with many such words, he exhorted them that they should remove his bones to Hebron, and that they should bury him with his fathers.

35. When he had eaten and drunken with a merry heart, he covered his face and died.

36. His sons did according to all that Naphtali their Father had commanded them.

THE TESTAMENT OF GAD

The Ninth Son of Jacob and Zilpah

Chapter 1

1. THE copy of the testament of Gad, what things he spoke to his sons, in the hundred and twenty-fifth year of his life, saying to them:

2. "Hearken, my children; I was the ninth son born to Jacob, and I was valiant in keeping the flocks.

3. Accordingly, I guarded the flock at night; and whenever the lion came, or the wolf, or any wild beast against the fold, I pursued it, and overtaking it, I seized its foot with my hand and hurled it about a stone's throw, and so killed it.

4. Now Joseph my brother was feeding the flock with us for upwards of thirty days, and being young, he fell sick by reason of the heat.

5. He returned to Hebron to our father, who made him lie down near him, because he loved him greatly.

6. Joseph told our father that the sons of Zilpah and Bilhah were slaying the best of the flock and eating them, against the judgement of Reuben and Judah.

7. For he saw that I had delivered a lamb out of the mouth of a bear, and put the bear to death; but I had slain the lamb, being grieved concerning it, because it could not live, and he told our father that we had eaten it.

8. Regarding this matter, I was angry with Joseph until the day that he was sold.

9. The spirit of hatred was in me, and I wished not either to hear of Joseph with the ears, or to see him with the eyes, because he rebuked us to our faces saying that we were eating of the flock without Judah.

10. For whatsoever things he told our father, our father believed him.

11. I confess now my kin, my children, that oftentimes I wished to kill him, because I hated him from my heart.

12. Moreover, I hated him yet more for his dreams; and I wished to lick him out of the land of the living, even as an ox licks up the grass of the field.

13. Judah sold him secretly to the Ishmaelites.

14. The God of our fathers delivered him from our hands, that we should not work great lawlessness in Israel.

15. Now, my children, hearken to the words of truth to work righteousness, and all the law of the Most High, and go not astray through the spirit of hatred, for it is evil in all the doings of men.

16. Whatsoever a man does, the hater despises him; and though a man works the law of the Lord, he praises him not; though a man fears the Lord, and takes pleasure in that which is righteous, the hater loves him not.

17. He scorns the truth; he envies him that prospers; he welcomes back-stabbing gossip; he loves arrogance; for hatred blinds his soul, as I also then looked on Joseph.

18. Beware, my children, of hatred, for it works lawlessness even against the Lord Himself.

19. For it will not hear the words of His commandments concerning the loving of one's neighbor, and it sins against God.

20. For if a brother stumbles, it delights immediately to proclaim it to all men, and is urgent that the object of his hatred should be judged for it, and to be punished, and to be put to death.

21. If hatred is in a servant, it stirs him up against his master, and with every affliction, it devises it against him, hoping, if possibly, he can be put to death.

22. For hatred works with envy against them that prosper, and so long as it hears of or sees their success, it always languishes.

23. For as love would quicken even the dead, and would call back them that are condemned to die, so hatred would slay the living, and those that had sinned in a manner that could otherwise be easily forgiven, it would not suffer them to live.

24. For the spirit of hatred works together with Satan, through hastiness of spirits, in all things to men's death; but the spirit of love works together with the law of God in long-suffering unto the salvation of men.

25. Hatred, therefore, is evil, for it constantly mates with lying, speaking against the truth; and it makes small things to be great, and causes the light to be darkness, and calls the sweet bitter, and teaches slander, and kindles wrath, and stirs up war and violence and all covetousness; it fills the heart with evils and devilish poison.

26. These things, therefore, I say to you from experience, my children, that you may drive out hatred, which is of the devil; and cleave to the love of God.

27. Righteousness casts out hatred, humility destroys envy.

28. For he that is just and humble is ashamed to do what is unjust, being reproved not of another, but of his own heart, because the Lord looks on his inclination.

29. He speaks not against a holy man, because the fear of God overcomes hatred.

30. For fearing lest he should offend the Lord, he will not do wrong to any man, even in thought.

31. These things I learned at last, after I had repented concerning Joseph.

32. For true repentance after a godly sort destroys ignorance, and drives away the darkness, and enlightens the eyes, and gives knowledge to the soul, and leads the mind to salvation.

33. Those things which it has not learned from man, it knows through repentance.

34. For God brought upon me a disease of the liver; and had not the prayers of Jacob my father succored me, it would have failed and my spirit departed.

35. For by what things a man transgresses, by the same also is he punished.

36. Since, therefore, my liver was set mercilessly against Joseph, in my liver too I suffered mercilessly, and I was judged for eleven months, for so long a time as I had been angry against Joseph.

Chapter 2

1. NOW, my children, I exhort you, love each one his brother, and put away hatred from your hearts, love one another in deed, and in word, and in the inclination of the soul.

2. For in the presence of my father, I spoke peaceably to Joseph; and when I had gone out, the spirit of hatred darkened my mind, and stirred up my soul to slay him.

3. Love one another from the heart; and if a man sins against you, speak peaceably to him, and in your soul, hold not guile; and if he repents and confesses, forgive him.

4. But if he denies it, do not get into a passion with him, lest catching the poison from you, he take to swearing, and so you sin doubly.

5. Let not another man hear your secrets when engaged in legal strife, lest he come to hate you and become your enemy and commit a great sin against you; for often times he addresses you guilefully, or he schemes with himself about you with wicked intent.

6. Though he denies it, and yet he has a sense of shame when reproved, give up reproving him.

7. For he who denies it may in fact repent, so as not to wrong you again; yes, he may also honor you, and fear, and be at peace with you.

8. If he is shameless and persists in his wrong-doing, even so forgive him from the heart, and leave to God the avenging.

9. If a man prospers more than you, do not be vexed, but pray also for him, that he may have perfect prosperity.

10. For so it is expedient for you.

11. If he is further exalted, don't be envious of him, remembering that all flesh shall die; and offer praise to God, who gives things good and profitable to all men.

12. Seek out the judgments of the Lord, and your mind will rest and be at peace.

13. Though a man becomes rich by evil means, even as Esau, the brother of my father, don't be jealous, but wait for the Lord's ending answer.

14. For if he takes away from a man wealth gotten by evil means, He forgives him if he repents, but the unrepentant is reserved for eternal punishment.

15. For the poor man, if free from envy, he pleases the Lord in all things, is blessed beyond all men, because he has not the travail of vain men.

16. Put away, therefore, jealousy from your souls, and love one another with uprightness of heart.

17. Tell these things to your children, that they honor Judah and Levi, for from them shall the Lord raise up salvation to Israel.

18. For I know that at the last, your children shall depart from Him, and shall walk in wickedness and affliction and corruption before the Lord."

19. When he had rested for a little while, he said again; "My children, obey your father, and bury me near to my fathers."

20. He drew up his feet and fell asleep in peace.

21. After five years, they carried him up to Hebron, and laid him with his fathers.

THE TESTAMENT OF ASHER

The Tenth Son of Jacob and Zilpah

Chapter 1

1. THE copy of the Testament To Asher, what things he spoke to his sons in the hundred and twenty-fifth year of his life.

2. For while he was still in health, he said to them: "Hearken, children of Asher, to your father, and I will declare to you all that is upright in the sight of the Lord.

3. Two ways has God given to the sons of men, and two inclinations, and two kinds of action, and two modes of action, and two issues.

4. Therefore all things are by twos, one over against the other.

5. For there are two ways of good and evil, and with these are the two inclinations in our breasts discriminating them.

135

6. Therefore, if the soul takes pleasure in the good inclination, all its actions are in righteousness; and if it sins, it straightway repents.

7. For, having its thoughts set upon righteousness, and casting away wickedness, it straightway overthrows the evil, and uproots the sin.

8. But if it inclines to the evil inclination, all its actions are in wickedness, and it drives away the good, and cleaves to the evil, and it is ruled by Satan; even though it works what is good, he perverts it to evil.

9. For whenever it begins to do good, he forces the issue of the action into evil for him, seeing that the treasure of the inclination is filled with an evil spirit.

10. A person then may, with words, help the good for the sake of the evil, yet the issue of the action leads to mischief.

11. There is a man who shows no compassion upon him who serves his turn in evil; and this thing has two aspects, but the whole is evil.

12. There is a man that loves him that works evil, because he would prefer even to die in evil for his sake; and concerning this, it is clear that it has two aspects, but the whole is an evil work.

13. Though indeed he has love, yet is he wicked who conceals what is evil for the sake of a good name, but the end of the action tends to evil.

14. Another steals, does unjustly, plunders, defrauds, but in spite of that, pities the poor; this too has a twofold aspect, but the whole is evil.

15. He who defrauds his neighbor provokes God, and swears falsely against the Most High, and yet pities the poor; the Lord who commanded the law, he sets aside and provokes, and yet he refreshes the poor.

16. He defiles the soul and makes gay the body, he kills many and pities few, this too has a twofold aspect, but the whole is evil.

17. Another commits adultery and fornication, and abstains from meats, and when he fasts, he does evil, and by the power of his wealth overwhelms many; and notwithstanding his excessive wickedness he does the commandments; this, too, has a twofold aspect, but the whole is evil.

18. Such men are hares; clean, like those that divide the hoof, but in deeds are unclean.

19. For God in the tables of the commandments has declared it.

20. But do not, my children, wear two faces like them, of goodness and of wickedness; but cleave to goodness only, for God has his habitation within it, and men desire it.

21. But from wickedness, flee away, destroying the evil inclination by your good works; for they that are double-faced serve not God but their own lusts, so that they may please Satan and men like themselves.

22. For good men, even they that are of single face, though they be thought by them that are double-faced to sin, are just before God.

23. For many in killing the wicked do two works, of good and evil; but the whole is good, because he has uprooted and destroyed that which is evil.

24. One man hates the merciful but unjust man, and the man who commits adultery but fasts: this, too, has a twofold aspect, but the whole work is good, because he follows the Lord's example, in that he accepts not the seeming good as the genuine good.

25. Another would rather not see good days with them that sin, lest they defile his body and pollute his soul; this, too, is double-faced, but the whole is good.

26. For such men are like to stags and to hinds, because in the manner of wild animals, they seem to be unclean, but they are altogether clean; because they walk in zeal for the Lord and abstain from what God also hates and forbids by

His commandments, warding off the evil from the good.

27. You see, my children, how there are two in all things, one against the other, and the one is hidden by the other: in wealth is hidden covetousness, in friendliness drunkenness, in laughter grief, in wedlock licentiousness.

28. Death succeeds to life, dishonor to glory, night to day, and darkness to light; and all things that are under the day, just things, are under life; but unjust things are under death; wherefore also eternal life awaits death.

29. Nor may it be said that truth is a lie, nor right wrong; for all truth is under the light, even as all things are under God.

30. All these things, therefore, I proved in my life, and I wandered not from the truth of the Lord, and I searched out the commandments of the Most High, walking according to all my strength with singleness of face to that which is good.

31. Take heed, therefore, you also, my children, to the commandments of the Lord, following the truth with singleness of face.

32. For they that are double-faced are guilty of a twofold sin; for they both do the evil thing and they have pleasure in them that do it, following the example of the spirits of deceit, and striving against mankind.

33. Therefore, my children, keep the law of the Lord, and give not heed to evil as to good; but look to the thing that is really good, and keep it in all commandments of the Lord, having your conversation therein, and resting therein.

34. For the latter end of men shows their righteousness or unrighteousness, when they meet the angels of the Lord and of Satan.

35. For when the soul that departs is troubled, it is tormented by the evil spirit which also it served in lusts and evil works.

36. But if he is peaceful with joy, he meets the angel of peace, and he leads him into eternal life.

37. Become not, my children, as Sodom, which sinned against the angels of the Lord, and perished forever.

38. For I know that you shall sin and be delivered into the hands of your enemies; and your land shall be made desolate, and your holy places destroyed, and you shall be scattered to the four corners of the earth.

39. You shall be set at nothing in the dispersion, vanishing away as water,

40. Until the Most High shall visit the earth, coming Himself as man, with men eating and drinking, and breaking the head of the dragon in the water.

41. He shall save Israel and all the Gentiles, God speaking in the person of man.

42. Therefore, my children, tell these things to your children, that they disobey Him not.

43. For I have known that you shall assuredly be disobedient and assuredly act ungodly, not giving heed to the law of God but to the

commandments of men, being corrupted through wickedness.

44. Therefore shall you be scattered as Gad and Dan, my brethren, and you shall know not your lands, tribe, and tongue.

45. But the Lord will gather you together in faith through His tender mercy, and for the sake of Abraham, Isaac, and Jacob."

46. When he had said these things to them, he commanded them, saying: "Bury me in Hebron."

47. He fell asleep and died at a good old age.

48. His sons did as he had commanded them, and they carried him up to Hebron, and buried him with his fathers.

THE TESTAMENT OF JOSEPH

The Eleventh Son of Jacob and Rachel

Chapter 1

1. THE copy of the Testament of Joseph.

2. When he was about to die, he called his sons and his brethren together, and he said to them:

3. "My brethren and my children, hearken to Joseph the beloved of Israel; give ear, my sons, to your father.

4. I have seen in my life envy and death, yet I went not astray, but I persevered in the truth of the Lord.

5. My brethren hated me, but the Lord loved me:

6. They wished to slay me, but the God of my fathers guarded me.

7. They let me down into a pit, and the Most High brought me up again.

8. I was sold into slavery, and the Lord of all made me free.

9. I was taken into captivity, and His strong hand succored me.

10. I was beset with hunger, and the Lord Himself nourished me.

11. I was alone, and God comforted me.

12. I was sick, and the Lord visited me.

13. I was in prison, and my God showed favor to me;

14. In bonds, and He released me;

15. Slandered, and He pleaded my cause;

16. Bitterly spoken against by the Egyptians, and He delivered me;

17. Envied by my fellow-slaves, and He exalted me.

18. The chief captain of Pharaoh entrusted to me his house,

19. And I struggled against a shameless woman, urging me to transgress with her; but the God of Israel my father delivered me from the burning flame.

20. I was cast into prison, I was beaten, I was mocked; but the Lord granted me to find mercy in the sight of the keeper of the prison.

21. For the Lord does not forsake them that fear Him, neither in darkness, nor in bonds, nor in tribulations, nor in necessities.

22. For God is not put to shame as a man, nor as the son of man is he afraid, nor as one that is earth-born is He weak or frighted.

23. But in all those things He gives protection, and in different ways, He comforts, though for a little space, He departs, to try the inclination of the soul.

24. In ten temptations, He showed me approved, and in all of them I endured; for endurance is a mighty charm, and patience gives many good things.

25. How often did the Egyptian woman threaten me with death!

26. How often did she give me over to punishment, and then call me back and threaten me, and when I was unwilling to company with her, she said to me:

27. 'You shall be lord of me, and all that is in my house, if you will give yourself to me, you shall be as our master.'

28. But I remembered the words of my father; and going into my chamber, I wept and prayed to the Lord.

29. I fasted in those seven years, and I appeared to the Egyptians as one living delicately, for they that fast for God's sake receive beauty of face.

30. If my lord was away from home, I drank no wine; and for three days, I did not take my food, but I gave it to the poor and sick.

31. I sought the Lord early, and I wept for the Egyptian woman of Memphis, for very

unceasingly did she trouble me, for also at night she came to me under pretense of visiting me.

32. Because she had no male child, she pretended to regard me as a son.

33. For a time, she embraced me as a son, and I knew it not; but later, she sought to draw me into fornication.

34. When I perceived it, I sorrowed unto death; and when she had gone out, I came to myself, and lamented for her many days, because I recognized her guile and her deceit.

35. I declared to her the words of the Most High, if haply she would turn from her evil lust.

36. Often, therefore, did she flatter me with words as a holy man, and guilefully in her talk praise my chastity before her husband, while desiring to ensnare me when we were alone.

37. For she lauded me openly as chaste, and in secret she said to me: 'Do not fear my husband; for he is persuaded concerning your chastity; for

even should one tell him concerning us, he would not believe.

38. Owing to all these things, I lay upon the ground and besought God that the Lord would deliver me from her deceit.

39. When she had prevailed nothing thereby, she came again to me under the plea of instruction, that she might learn the word of God.

40. She said to me: 'If you will that I should leave my idols, lie with me, and I will persuade my husband to depart from his idols, and we will walk in the law by your Lord.'

41. I said to her: 'The Lord wills not that those who reverence Him should be in uncleanness, nor does He take pleasure in them that commit adultery, but in those that approach Him with a pure heart and undefiled lips.'

42. But she bided her time, longing to accomplish her evil desire.

43. I gave myself yet more to fasting and prayer, that the Lord might deliver me from her.

44. Again, at another time, she said to me: 'If you will not commit adultery, I will kill my husband by poison; and take you to be my husband.'

45. I therefore, when I heard this, rent my garments, and said to her:

46. 'Woman, reverence God, and don't do this evil deed, lest you be destroyed; for know, indeed, that I will declare this, your device, to all men.'

47. She therefore, being afraid, besought that I would not declare this device.

48. She departed, soothing me with gifts, and sending to me every delight of the sons of men.

49. Afterwards, she sent me food mingled with enchantments.

50. When the eunuch who brought it came to me, I looked up and beheld a terrible man

giving me the dish of a sword, and I perceived that her scheme was to beguile me.

51. When he had gone out, I wept, and I did not taste that or any other of her food.

52. So then after one day, she came to me and observed the food, and she said to me: 'Why is it that you have not eaten of the food?'

53. I said to her: 'It is because you have filled it with deadly enchantments; and you said, I come not near to idols but to the Lord alone.

54. Now therefore, know that the God of my father has revealed to me by His angel your wickedness, and I have kept it to convict you, if haply you may see and repent.

55. But that you may learn that the wickedness of the ungodly has no power over them that worship God with chastity, I will take of it and eat before you.'

56. Having so said, I prayed: 'The God of my fathers and the angel of Abraham, be with me,' and I ate.

57. When she saw this, she fell upon her face at my feet, weeping; and I raised her up and admonished her.

58. She promised to do this iniquity no more.

59. But her heart was still set on evil, and she looked around for how to ensnare me, and sighing deeply, she became downcast, though she was not sick.

60. When her husband saw her, he said to her: 'Why has your countenance fallen?'

61. She said to him: 'I have a pain at my heart, and the groaning of my spirit oppresses me,' and so he comforted her who was not sick.

62. Then, accordingly, seizing an opportunity, she rushed to me while her husband was yet without, and said to me: 'I will hang myself or cast myself over a cliff if you will not lie with me.'

63. When I saw the spirit of Satan was troubling her, I prayed to the Lord, and I said to her:

64. 'Why, wretched woman, are you troubled and disturbed, blinded through sins?

65. Remember that if you kill yourself, Asteho, the concubine of your husband, your rival, will beat your children, and you will destroy your memorial from off the earth.

66. She said to me: 'Then you love me; let this suffice me; only strive for my life and my children, and I expect that I shall enjoy my desire also.'

67. But she knew not that because of my lord, I spoke thus, and not because of her.

68. For if a man has fallen before the passion of a wicked desire and becomes enslaved by it, even as she was, whatever good thing he may hear with regard to that passion, he receives it with a positive view to his wicked desire.

69. I declare, therefore, to you, my children, that it was about the sixth hour when she departed from me; and I knelt before the Lord all day and

all night; and about dawn I rose up, weeping the while and praying for a release from her.

70. At last, then, she laid hold of my garments, forcibly dragging me to have relations with her.

71. When, therefore, I saw that in her madness she was holding fast to my garment, I left it behind, and fled away naked.

72. Holding fast to the garment, she falsely accused me, and when her husband came, he cast me into prison in his house; and the next day, he scourged me and sent me into Pharaoh's prison.

73. When I was in bonds, the Egyptian woman was oppressed with grief, and she came and heard how I gave thanks to the Lord and sang praises in the abode of darkness, and with glad voice rejoiced, glorifying my God that I was delivered from the lustful desire of the Egyptian woman.

74. Often had she sent to me saying: 'Consent to fulfill my desire, and I will release you from

your bonds, and I will free you from the darkness.'

75. And not even in thought did I incline to her.

76. For God loves him, who in a den of wickedness, combines fasting with chastity, rather than the man who in kings' chambers combines luxury with license.

77. If a man lives in chastity, and desires also glory, and the Most High knows that it is

expedient for him, He bestows this also upon him.

78. How often, though she were sick, did she come down to me at unlooked for times, and listened to my voice as I prayed!

79. When I heard her groaning, I held my peace.

80. For when I was in her house, she was wont to bare her arms and breasts and legs, that I might lie with her; for she was very beautiful, splendidly adorned, in order to beguile me.

81. The Lord guarded me from her devices.

Chapter 2

1. YOU see, therefore, my children, what great things patience works, and prayer with fasting.

2. So you too, if you follow after chastity and purity with patience and prayer, with fasting in humility of heart, the Lord will dwell among you, because He loves chastity.

3. Wheresoever the Most High dwells, even though envy, or slavery, or slander befalls a man, the Lord who dwells in him, for the sake of his chastity, not only delivers him from evil, but also exalts him, even as me.

4. For in every way, the man is lifted up, whether in deed or in word or in thought.

5. My brethren knew how my father loved me, and yet I did not exalt myself in my mind; although I was a child, I had the fear of God in

my heart; for I knew that all things would pass away.

6. I did not raise myself against them with evil intent, but I honored my brethren; and out of respect for them, even when I was being sold, I refrained from telling the Ishmaelites that I was a son of Jacob, a great man and a mighty man.

7. You also, my children, have the fear of God in all of your works before your eyes, and honor your brethren.

8. For everyone who does the law of the Lord shall be loved by Him.

9. When I came to the Indocolpitae with the Ishmaelites, they asked me, saying:

10. 'Are you a slave?' I told them that I was a home-born slave, that I might not put my brethren to shame.

11. The eldest of them said to me: 'You are not a slave, for even your appearance makes it manifest.'

12. But I said that I was their slave.

13. Now when we came into Egypt, they strove concerning me, which of them should buy me and take me.

14. Therefore it seemed good to all that I should remain in Egypt with the merchant of their trade, until they should return bringing merchandise.

15. The Lord gave me favor in the eyes of the merchant, and he entrusted to me his house.

16. God blessed him by my means, and increased him in gold and silver and in household servants.

17. I was with him three months and five days.

18. About that time, the Memphian woman, the wife of Pentephris, came down in a chariot with great pomp, because she had heard from her eunuchs concerning me.

19. She told her husband that the merchant had become rich by means of a young Hebrew, and

they say that he had assuredly been stolen out of the land of Canaan.

20. Now, therefore, render justice to him, and take away the youth to your house; so shall the God of the Hebrews bless you, for grace from heaven is upon him.

21. Pentephris was persuaded by her words, and commanded the merchant to be brought, and said to him:

22. 'What is this that I hear concerning you, that you steal persons out of the land of Canaan, and sell them for slaves?'

23. But the merchant fell at his feet and besought him, saying: 'I beseech you, my lord, I know not what you say.'

24. Pentephris said to him: 'From where, then, is the Hebrew slave?'

25. He said: 'The Ishmaelites entrusted him to me until they should return.'

26. But he did not believe him, but he commanded him to be stripped and beaten.

27. When he persisted in this statement, Pentephris said: 'Let the youth be brought.'

28. When I was brought in, I did homage to Pentephris, for he was third in rank of the officers of Pharaoh.

29. He took me apart from him, and he said to me: 'Are you a slave or free?'

30. I said: 'A slave.'

31. He said: 'Whose?'

32. I said: 'The Ishmaelites'.'

33. He said: 'How did you become their slave?'

34. I said: 'They bought me out of the land of Canaan.'

35. He said to me: 'Truly you lie,' and straightway, he commanded me to be stripped and beaten.

36. Now, the Memphian woman was looking through a window at me while I was being beaten, for her house was near, and she sent to him saying:

37. 'Your judgement is unjust; for you punish a free man who has been stolen, as though he were a transgressor.'

38. When I made no change in my statement, though I was beaten, he ordered me to be imprisoned, until, he said, the owners of the boy should come.

39. The woman said to her husband: 'Why do you detain the captive and wellborn lad in bonds, who ought rather to be set at liberty, and be waited upon?'

40. For she wished to see me out of a desire of sin, but I was ignorant concerning all these things.

41. He said to her: 'It is not the custom of the Egyptians to take that which belongs to others before proof is given.'

42. This, therefore, he said concerning the merchant; but as for the lad, 'he must be imprisoned.'

43. Now after four and twenty days came the Ishmaelites, for they had heard that Jacob my father was mourning much concerning me.

44. They came and said to me: 'How is it that you said that you were a slave? We have learned that you are the son of a mighty man in the land of Canaan, and your father still mourns for you in sackcloth and ashes.'

45. When I heard this, my bowels were dissolved and my heart melted, and I desired greatly to weep, but I restrained myself that I should not put my brethren to shame.

46. I said to them, 'I know not, I am a slave.'

47. Then, therefore, they took counsel to sell me, that I should not be found in their hands.

48. For they feared my father, lest he should come and execute upon them a grievous vengeance.

49. For they had heard that he was mighty with God and with men.

50. Then said the merchant to them: 'Release me from the judgement of Pentiphri.'

51. They came and requested me, saying: 'Say that you were bought by us with money, and he will set us free.'

52. Now the Memphian woman said to her husband: 'Buy the youth; for I hear, said she, that they are selling him.'

53. Straightway she sent a eunuch to the Ishmaelites and asked them to sell me.

54. But since the eunuch would not agree to buy me at their price, he returned, having made trial of them, and he made known to his mistress that they asked a large price for their slave.

55. She sent another eunuch, saying: 'Even though they demand two minas, give it to them, do not spare the gold; only buy the boy and bring him to me.'

56. The eunuch therefore went and gave them eighty pieces of gold, and he received me; but to the Egyptian woman, he said I have given a hundred.

57. Though I knew this, I held my peace, lest the eunuch should be put to shame.

58. You see, therefore, my children, what great things I endured that I should not put my brethren to shame.

59. You do also, therefore, love one another, and with long-suffering, hide one another's faults.

60. For God delights in the unity of brethren, and in the purpose of a heart that takes pleasure in love.

61. When my brethren came into Egypt, they learned that I had returned their money to them, and upbraided them not and comforted them.

62. After the death of Jacob, my father, I loved them more abundantly, and all things whatsoever he commanded, I did very abundantly for them.

63. I suffered them not to be afflicted in the smallest matter; and all that was in my hand, I gave to them.

64. Their children were my children, and my children as their servants; and their life was my life, and all their suffering was my suffering, and all their sickness was my infirmity.

65. My land was their land, and their counsel my counsel.

66. I exalted not myself among them in arrogance because of my worldly glory, but I was among them as one of the least.

67. If you also, therefore, walk in the commandments of the Lord, my children, He will exalt you there, and will bless you with good things for ever and ever.

68. If anyone seeks to do evil to you, do well to him, and pray for him, and you shall be redeemed of the Lord from all evil.

69. For, behold, you see that out of my humility and longsuffering I took unto wife the daughter of the priest of Heliopolis.

70. A hundred talents of gold were given to me with her, and the Lord made them to serve me.

71. He gave me also beauty as a flower beyond the beautiful ones of Israel; and He preserved me to old age in strength and in beauty, because I was like in all things to Jacob.

72. Hear, my children, also the vision which I saw.

73. There were twelve harts feeding, and the nine were first dispersed over all the earth, and likewise also the three.

74. I saw that from Judah was born a virgin wearing a linen garment, and from her was born a lamb, without spot; and on his left hand there was as it were a lion; and all the beasts rushed against him, and the lamb overcame them, and destroyed them and trod them under foot.

75. Because of him, the angels and men rejoiced, and all the land.

76. These things shall come to pass in their season, in the last days.

77. Therefore, my children, observe the commandments of the Lord, and honor Levi and Judah; for from them shall arise unto you the Lamb of God, who takes away the sin of the world, one who saves all the Gentiles and Israel.

78. For His kingdom is an everlasting kingdom, which shall not pass away; but my kingdom among you shall come to an end as a watcher's hammock, which after the summer disappears.

79. For I know that after my death, the Egyptians will afflict you, but God will avenge you, and will bring you into that which He promised to your fathers.

80. But you shall carry up my bones with you; for when my bones are being taken up there, the Lord shall be with you in light, and Satan shall be in darkness with the Egyptians.

81. Carry up Asenath your mother to the Hippodrome, and near Rachel your mother bury her."

82. When he had said these things, he stretched out his feet and died at a good old age.

83. All Israel mourned for him, and all Egypt, with a great mourning.

84. When the children of Israel went out of Egypt, they took with them the bones of Joseph, and they buried him in Hebron with his fathers, and the years of his life were one hundred and ten years.

THE TESTAMENT OF BENJAMIN

The Twelfth Son of Jacob and Rachel

Chapter 1

1. THE copy of the words of Benjamin, which he commanded his sons to observe, after he had lived a hundred and twenty-five years.

2. He kissed them and said: "As Isaac was born to Abraham in his old age, so also was I to Jacob.

3. Since Rachel my mother died in giving me birth, I had no milk; therefore I was suckled by Bilhah her handmaid.

4. For Rachel remained barren for twelve years after she had borne Joseph; and she prayed to the Lord with fasting twelve days, and she conceived and bare Me.

5. For my father loved Rachel dearly, and prayed that he might see two sons born from her.

6. Therefore was I called Benjamin, that is, a son of days.

7. When I went into Egypt, to Joseph, and my brother recognized me, he said to me: 'What did they tell my father when they sold me?'

8. I said to him: 'They dabbled your coat with blood and sent it, and they said, "Do you know whether this is your son's coat?"'

9. He said to me: 'Even so, brother, when they had stripped me of my coat, they gave me to the Ishmaelites, and they gave me a loin cloth, and scourged me, and commanded me to run.

10. And as for one of them that had beaten me with a rod, a lion met him and slew him.

11. So his associates were frightened.'

12. So you, therefore, my children, love the Lord God of heaven and earth, and keep His commandments, following the example of the good and holy man Joseph.

13. Let your mind be good, even as you know me; for he that has his mind right, sees all things rightly.

14. Fear the Lord, and love your neighbor; and even though the spirits of Satan claim you, to afflict you with every evil, yet shall they not have dominion over you, even as they had not over Joseph my brother.

15. How many men wished to slay him, and God shielded him!

16. For he that fears God and loves his neighbor cannot be smitten by the spirit of Satan, being shielded by the fear of God.

17. Nor can he be ruled over by the device of men or beasts, for he is helped by the Lord through the love which he has towards his neighbor.

18. For Joseph also besought our father that he would pray for his brethren, that the Lord would not impute to them as sin whatever evil they had done to him.

19. So Jacob cried out: 'My good child, you have prevailed over the bowels of your father Jacob.'

20. He embraced him, and kissed him for two hours, saying:

21. 'In you shall be fulfilled the prophecy of heaven concerning the Lamb of God, and Savior of the world, and that a blameless one shall be delivered up for lawless men, and a sinless one shall die for ungodly men in the blood of the covenant, for the salvation of the Gentiles and of Israel, and shall destroy Satan and his servants.'

22. See, therefore, my children, the end of the good man?

23. Be followers of his compassion, therefore, with a good mind, that you also may wear crowns of glory.

24. For the good man has not a dark eye; for he shows mercy to all men, even though they are sinners.

25. Though they devise with evil intent concerning him, by doing good, he overcomes

evil, being shielded by God; and he loves the righteous as his own soul.

26. If anyone is glorified, he envies him not; if anyone is enriched, he is not jealous; if anyone is valiant, he praises him; the virtuous man he lauds; on the poor man he has mercy; on the weak, he has compassion; unto God he sings praises.

27. He that has the grace of a good spirit, he loves as his own soul.

28. If therefore, you also have a good mind, then will both wicked men be at peace with you, and the profligate will reverence you and turn to good; and the covetous will not only cease from their inordinate desire, but even give the objects of their covetousness to them that are afflicted.

29. If you do well, even the unclean spirits will flee from you; and the beasts will dread you.

30. For where there is reverence for good works and light in the mind, even darkness flees away from him.

31. For if anyone does violence to a holy man, he repents; for the holy man is merciful to his reviler, and holds his peace.

32. If anyone betrays a righteous man, the righteous man prays; though for a little he is humbled, yet not long after, he appears far more glorious, as was Joseph my brother.

33. The inclination of the good man is not in the power of the deceit of the spirit of Satan, for the angel of peace guides his soul.

34. He gazes not passionately upon corruptible things, nor gathers together riches through a desire of pleasure.

35. He delights not in pleasure, he grieves not his neighbor, he satisfies not himself with luxuries, he errs not in the uplifting of the eyes, for the Lord is his portion.

36. The good inclination receives not glory or dishonor from men, and it knows not any guile or lie or fighting or reviling; for the Lord dwells

in him and lights up his soul, and he rejoices towards all men always.

37. The good mind has not two tongues, of blessing and of cursing, of contumely and of honor, of sorrow and of joy, of quietness and of confusion, of hypocrisy and of truth, of poverty and of wealth; but it has one disposition, uncorrupt and pure, concerning all men.

38. It has no double sight, nor double hearing; for in everything which he does, or speaks, or sees, he knows that the Lord looks on his soul.

39. He cleanses his mind that he may not be condemned by men as well as by God.

40. In like manner, the works of Satan are twofold, and there is no singleness in them.

41. Therefore, my children, I tell you, flee the malice of Satan; for he gives a sword to them that obey him.

42. The sword is the mother of seven evils. First the mind conceives through Satan, and first there is bloodshed; secondly ruin; thirdly,

tribulation; fourthly, exile; fifthly, lack; sixthly, panic; seventhly, destruction.

43. Therefore was Cain also delivered over to seven vengeances by God, for in every hundred years, the Lord brought one plague upon him.

44. When he was two hundred years old, he began to suffer, and in the nine-hundredth year, he was destroyed.

45. For on account of Abel, his brother, with all of the evils, was he judged, but Lamech with seventy times seven.

46. Because forever, those who are like Cain in envy and hatred of brethren, shall be punished with the same judgement."

Chapter 2

1. MY children, flee evil-doing, envy, and hatred of brethren, and cleave to goodness and love.

2. He that has a pure mind in love, looks not after a woman with a view to fornication; for he has no defilement in his heart, because the Spirit of God rests upon him.

3. For as the sun is not defiled by shining on dung and mire, but rather dries up both and drives away the evil smell, so also the pure mind, though encompassed by the defilements of earth, rather cleanses them and is not itself defiled.

4. I believe that there will be also evil-doings among you, from the words of Enoch the righteous: that you shall commit fornication with the fornication of Sodom, and shall perish, all save a few, and shall renew wanton deeds with women; and the kingdom of the Lord shall not be among you, for straightway He shall take it away.

5. Nevertheless, the temple of God shall be in your portion, and the last temple shall be more glorious than the first.

6. The twelve tribes shall be gathered together there, and all the Gentiles, until the Most High shall send forth His salvation in the visitation of an only-begotten prophet.

7. He shall enter into the first temple, and there shall the Lord be treated with outrage, and He shall be lifted up upon a tree.

8. The veil of the temple shall be rent, and the Spirit of God shall pass on to the Gentiles as fire poured forth.

9. He shall ascend from Hades and shall pass from earth into heaven.

10. I know how lowly He shall be upon earth, and how glorious in heaven.

11 Now when Joseph was in Egypt, I longed to see his figure and the form of his countenance; and through the prayers of Jacob my father, I

saw him, while awake in the daytime, even his entire figure exactly as he was."

12. When he had said these things, he said to them: "Know, therefore, my children, that I am dying.

13. Tell the truth, each one to his neighbor, and keep the law of the Lord and His commandments.

14. For these things do I leave to you instead of inheritance.

15. Also, these words, give them to your children for an everlasting possession; for so did both Abraham, and Isaac, and Jacob.

16. For all these things they gave us for an inheritance, saying: 'Keep the commandments of God, until the Lord shall reveal His salvation to all Gentiles."

17. Then shall you see Enoch, Noah, and Shem, and Abraham, and Isaac, and Jacob, rising on the right hand in gladness,

18. Then shall we also rise, each one over our tribe, worshipping the King of heaven, who appeared upon earth in the form of a man in humility.

19. As many as believe on Him on the earth shall rejoice with Him.

20. Then also, all men shall rise, some to glory and some to shame.

21. The Lord shall judge Israel first for their unrighteousness; for when He appeared as God in the flesh to deliver them, they believed Him not.

22. Then shall He judge all the Gentiles, as many as believed Him not when He appeared upon earth.

23. He shall convict Israel through the chosen ones of the Gentiles, even as He reproved Esau through the Midianites, who deceived their brethren, so that they fell into fornication and idolatry; and they were alienated from God,

becoming therefore children in the portion of them that do not fear the Lord.

24. If you therefore, my children, walk in holiness according to the commandments of the Lord, you shall again dwell securely with me, and all Israel shall be gathered to the Lord.

25. I shall no longer be called a ravening wolf on account of your ravages, but a worker of the Lord, distributing food to them that work what is good.

26. There shall arise in the latter days one beloved of the Lord, of the tribe of Judah and Levi, a doer of His good pleasure in his mouth, with new knowledge enlightening the Gentiles.

27. Until the consummation of the age shall he be in the synagogues of the Gentiles, and among their rulers, as a strain of music in the mouth of all.

28. He shall be inscribed in the holy books, both his work and his word, and he shall be a chosen one of God forever.

29. Through them, he shall go to and fro as Jacob my father, saying: 'He shall fill up that which lacks of your tribe.'"

30. And when he had said these things, he stretched out his feet,

31. And died in a beautiful and good sleep.

32. His sons did as he had enjoined them, and they took up his body and buried it in Hebron with his fathers.

33. The number of the days of his life was a hundred and twenty-five years.

entirely JESUS

Praise the Lord!

See more at:
EntirelyJesus.com

Made in United States
Troutdale, OR
07/26/2023

11566127R00104